Family Fun Nights

Family Fun Nights

140 Activities the Whole Family Will Enjoy

Lisa Bany-Winters

CHICAGO
REVIEW
PRESS

Library of Congress Cataloging-in-Publication Data

Bany-Winters, Lisa.

 Family fun nights : 140 activities the whole family will enjoy / Lisa Bany-Winters.--
1st ed.

   p. cm.
 ISBN-13: 978-1-55652-608-4
 ISBN-10: 1-55652-608-3
1. Family recreation. I. Title.
 GV182.8.B36 2006
 790.1'91--dc22

                    2005034371

Cover design and illustration: Sheree Boyd
Interior illustration: Laura D'Argo
Interior design: Sarah Olson

© 2006 by Lisa Bany-Winters
All rights reserved
First edition
Published by Chicago Review Press, Incorporated
814 North Franklin Street
Chicago, Illinois 60610
ISBN-13: 978-1-55652-608-4
ISBN-10: 1-55652-608-3
Printed in the United States of America
5 4 3 2 1

This book is dedicated with love to my first family: Nancy, John, and Martin and my second family: Brian, Michaela, and Carlin for sharing with me the importance of family

Contents

Acknowledgments

Contributing author: Brian Winters, Naturalist for the Cook County Forest Preserves, for Indoor Garden Night and Science Night chapters.

I would like to thank the following people who have taught me, played with me, and inspired me to write this book: Joseph Albright, Josh Andrews, Suzy Andrews, John and Nancy Bany, Martin and Sarah Bany, Michaela Bany-Winters, Geoff Coates, Martin de Maat, Jayme Ernsteen, Melanie Gordon, Amy Harmon, Kristie Hassinger, Janine and Theresa Hedges, J. Casey Lane, the Leja Family, Jeff Lisse, Barbara Kanady, Laura Maloney, Anthony and Dana McKinney, Northlight Theatre Academy students, Laura Pekarek, Betty and Russell Pobst, Leigh Anna Reichenbach, Stephanie Repin, Danny Robles, J. R. Rose, the Schwartzman Family, the Schwendeman Family, Brian Shively, Klahr Thorsen, and Amy Weiss.

I would like to thank the staff of Chicago Review Press, including Gerilee Hundt, managing editor; Allison Felus, production editor; Jon Hahn, editorial assistant; Sharon Sofinski, copyeditor; Sheree Boyd, cover illustrator and designer; Laura D'Argo, interior illustrator; and Sarah Olson, interior page production artist. I'd also like to thank Cynthia Sherry, associate publisher, for the continuing opportunities; and Lisa Rosenthal, my book editor, for all of her creativity, ideas, input and magic!

Introduction to Parents

A recent article in *Forever Families* included the findings from a national study of 1,500 schoolchildren who were asked what makes a happy family. Children didn't list things such as money or fancy cars. The most common answer was doing things together as a family. Spending time together can also be good for your health—it's been shown that an enjoyable family evening can boost your immune system for days.

Family memories and traditions can be created in an evening without a lot of work, and these memories can last a lifetime. *Family Fun Nights* is written for parents who want to help enhance family time. Families are very busy, with competing schedules and demands on everyone's time, so when you do have time together, you don't want to waste any of it preparing for fun. *Family Fun Nights* activities require little or no preparation. Perhaps you have a little time after dinner or just before bedtime, or perhaps your child's Little League game was just rained out. These are all perfect times to enjoy family time, and making time for building fun family memories is the goal of this book.

Family Fun Nights is for working parents, divorced parents, grandparents, and anyone looking for great ideas for making the most out of family time.

> The *Mom Central* newsletter suggests you "establish family traditions that take precedence over outside activities, no matter how busy each family member becomes. Make spending time together a priority." Your children will be glad you did.

> "It is hard to hurry up while skipping stones or watching a garden grow. Spend time together . . . giggle a little."
> —Peggy North-Jones, family educational consultant

❊ Laugh together with Giggle Night, Sticky Icky Night, Splash Night, and Opposite Night.

❊ Explore nature with your family during Animal Night, Indoor Garden Night, and Science Night, which feature fun and educational activities.

❊ Pamper yourselves with Spa Night, Formal Night, or Jewelry Night.

❊ Even camera-shy families will smile about Talent Night, Circus Night, Poetry Slam Night, and Movie Star Night.

❊ Or scare yourselves silly with Spooky Night, Mystery Night, and Fortune-Telling Night.

❊ Create treasures and memories for years to come with Scrapbook Night and Family History Night.

❊ Celebrate any day with Happy Unbirthday Night, Create-Your-Own Holiday Night, Winter in July Night, or Summer in January Night.

Any night you spend together, no matter what activities you choose, will be a positively fun experience for everyone!

Not sure what group of activities to choose? Open *Family Fun Nights* to the Contents page, close your eyes, point to an activity, and jump into the fun with your family.

Talent Night

Everybody has a talent for something. Why not spend an evening tapping into your family's talents? You may even discover a hidden talent in yourself or another family member.

Performing in front of each other will build self-confidence and make you more comfortable when doing a class presentation at school. Just pretend the folks watching you are members of your own family who love you—then you're sure to shine.

To set the mood for Talent Night, find a couple of objects you can use as microphones, such as a hairbrush or an empty toilet paper roll. Transform an area in your house into a stage and get ready to perform! Talent Night is sure to have you singing, acting, dancing, and laughing out loud together—a perfect family evening.

Variety Show

This is a favorite at my house. Family members take turns performing anything they want for each other. Here are some ideas:

✳ Turn on some classical music and do a ballet dance—real or funny. If you have a tutu, put it on!

✳ Sing your favorite song.

✳ Turn on a recording of your favorite song and lip-sync to it.

✳ Play an instrument. If you don't have one, you can put some tissue over a comb and hum through it like a kazoo.

✳ Turn on some fun dance music and make up a dance.

✳ Read or recite a poem. (See Poetry Slam Night for ideas on a poem to recite.)

✳ Tell a short story.

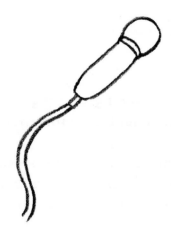

Here's an example of a short story you can tell for your part of the show. This is called "Mrs. Large Mouth Toad." Whenever Mrs. Large Mouth Toad talks, you open your mouth as wide as you can.

Once upon a time Mrs. Large Mouth Toad had a baby. It was her first baby, and she didn't know what to feed it. She decided to ask some other animals for advice. First, she went up to Mrs. Bear and said, "Mrs. Bear, I just had a baby. What do you feed your baby?"

Mrs. Bear grumbled and said, "I feed my baby nuts and berries, but that's not right for your baby. Why don't you go ask Mrs. Giraffe?"

So Mrs. Large Mouth Toad hopped over to Mrs. Giraffe and said, "Mrs. Giraffe, I just had a baby. What do you feed your baby?"

Mrs. Giraffe giggled and said, "I feed my baby leaves from the tallest trees, but that's not right for your baby. Why don't you go ask Mrs. Alligator?"

So Mrs. Large Mouth Toad hopped over to Mrs. Alligator and said, "Mrs. Alligator, I just had a baby. What do you feed your baby?"

Mrs. Alligator said, "Large Mouth Toads."

"Oh, really?" said Mrs. Large Mouth Toad (with her mouth as small as possible), and she hopped away.

Skits

It's fun to act out skits and short plays with your family. Here are some ideas to help you create original skits.

Choose a favorite story that everyone knows, decide who will play each part, and act it out. Some stories everyone knows include *Goldilocks and the Three Bears*, *The Three Little Pigs*, and *Little Red Riding Hood*. You can make up your own funny version of these stories by changing some details. For example, you can have the three bears eat your family's favorite meal instead of porridge, or add to the "Grandmother, what big eyes you have" part by telling her things such as "What big hands you have," "What big feet you have," or "What big shoulders you have." Grandma can respond with silly answers like "The better to wave to you, my dear," "The better to dance with you, my dear," or "The better to give you a piggyback ride!"

Divide your family into two teams and have each team give the other team three words. You then have five minutes to create a skit that uses all three of the words given to you by the other team. Perform your skits for each other.

Everyone choose a favorite character to play from any book, cartoon, movie, or television show. Act out a skit about these characters meeting. What would they say to each other? Do they have things in common? Would they get along? For example, suppose one person chooses to play Dorothy from *The Wizard of Oz*, one person chooses Bugs Bunny, one person chooses Harry Potter, and one person chooses Captain Hook. Would Dorothy, Harry Potter, and Captain Hook compare their fantasy worlds? Would Captain Hook recruit Bugs Bunny to make mischief with him? Would Dorothy and Harry Potter become friends?

Sing-Along

You don't have to have a beautiful voice, just a willingness to have fun. Here are some ideas to make your sing-along harmonious!

> Many bands consist of family members who like to make music together. One example is the Beach Boys, a band made up of three brothers, a cousin, and a friend of the family.

1. Think of a word or subject, then try to sing as many songs as you can that include that word or that focus on that subject. Here are some words and subject suggestions:

   * Love   * The sun   * Girl names
   * Snow   * Farms   * Boy names
   * Insects   * Animals   * Trains

2. Take turns choosing the song. When it's your turn, try to pick a song everyone knows. It's most fun when everyone can sing along.

You can collect all these funny and fun songs and make a family songbook. Write down the lyrics to your version of a song and collect sheet music for the songs your family likes to sing. If someone in your family can read music and play an instrument, that's even better. Otherwise, use one of the Unusual Orchestra instruments you create in the next activity to keep time while you sing. Keep the lyrics and sheet music together in a binder or folder. Then whenever someone pulls out the family songbook, you know it's time for a sing-along!

Unusual Orchestra

In this activity you make music with objects found around your house. You'll be surprised how many you'll be able to find. Find an object and decide how to play it. Here are some ideas:

✴ Upside-down pots become drums.

✴ Pot lids become cymbals.

✴ A cheese grater makes a cool sound when scraped with a spoon.

✴ Two spoons together can be used to make all sorts of fun rhythms.

✴ Cardboard boxes make good drums.

✴ Blow into a bottle with liquid inside to make a whistle sound. Try different kinds of bottles with different amounts of liquid to discover all the different tones you can make.

✴ Fill glasses with different amounts of water and tap them with a spoon. Be careful not to tap too hard!

Once everyone has found a household instrument to play, have a jam session. Start making sounds with your instrument by banging it, shaking it, or tapping it using a pattern such as this: shake it, then stop and count to one, then shake it again. Or try another pattern: tap the instrument, stop and count to three, then tap it again, repeating the same pattern. These are called rhythmic patterns. See how long you can keep your rhythmic pattern going. Try playing alone and then with other members of your household band.

A real orchestra is made up of families of instruments including strings, woodwinds, brass, percussion, and keyboards. Can you guess what instruments are in each family?

When you all play together you'll find new sound patterns that might inspire you to change your rhythmic pattern, so do it. Let each family member take a solo where they get to play their instrument alone while everyone else silently counts to 32.

After practicing and playing around for a while, try playing a song together. You can use the glasses or bottles to try to play something simple such as "Mary Had a Little Lamb," or you can sing along and play something such as "I've Been Working on the Railroad." See if you can make some of the instruments imitate the sounds of a train.

For variation, play call and respond. Take turns being the leader. The leader plays a rhythm with her instrument, and then the others respond by repeating the same rhythm back.

Paper Bag Maracas

If there are no instruments in your house, you can make your own!

What You Need

* Paper bags
* Markers or stickers to decorate
* Dry rice or beans
* Yarn

1. Use the markers or stickers to decorate
2. Place a handful of rice or beans in each bag.
3. Tie yarn around each bag about halfway down. Be sure to tie it tight so the rice or beans won't fall out.
4. Gently hold (don't squeeze) the bags under the yarn and shake.

If you're not sure what music to shake your maracas to, try Mexican or Spanish music. The Mexican Hat Dance is fun. You can place a hat in the middle of the room and dance around it as you shake your maracas.

> Maracas are percussion instruments that were first used by the Native Indians of Puerto Rico.

Your Song

Do you know any songs that have someone's name in the lyrics? Try putting your family members' names in it instead! You'd be surprised how well you can make it work. Sing a song like "Mary Had a Little Lamb," but put your name in it and put something else in place of the lamb. Here's an example:

> *Tony had a little phone, little phone, little phone,*
> *Tony had a little phone, and he was very proud.*
> *But everywhere that Tony went, Tony went, Tony went,*
> *Everywhere that Tony went, his phone would ring too loud!*

You also can create your own song that includes the names of all your family members, including your pets. Pick a theme, such as love, and make the song about the ways you love your family and show them that you love them, too.

See who can sing their song the loudest or the softest, or hold the longest note.

Circus Night

Tonight, run away with the circus (and your family) without ever leaving your home. A circus has many different acts performed by people of all ages, plus animals.

Many circus acts are family acts. Children learn the tricks and talents of the trade from their parents, and they often perform together. Even if you're not a gymnast, you can have fun clowning around with your family on Circus Night.

There are tricks to do and treats to eat. You can fly, walk across a tightrope, train animals, or even pretend to be an animal. So put on your clown face, have a parade, and enjoy Circus Night. To set the mood, play circus music if you have it. If not, any upbeat music will do.

Circus Tricks

Take turns having each family member choose a circus trick to perform. Here are some ideas:

Juggle. If you can't juggle balls, try juggling scarves. Take three small, lightweight scarves and toss them one at a time into the air. As you toss one, catch another. The light weight of the scarves makes them easy to juggle, and the trick looks great, too.

Balance. Try balancing different things in the palm of your hand. Things that are long work best, such as a broomstick or an umbrella, but be careful and make sure you have a lot of room. Also try balancing things on your head. See how many light books you can put on your head and how many steps you can take without the books falling.

Do gymnastics. If you have room and weather permits, go outside to do cartwheels, somersaults, and more. You can also make a human pyramid. Just make sure an adult is present to supervise. To make a pyramid with six people, the three largest people go on the ground on their hands and knees, then two people go on top of them, then the smallest person goes on the very top. To make a pyramid with three people, have two larger people stand next to each other with their knees bent a little toward each other. Then have the smaller person balance standing on their knees. Be sure to end your trick with "Ta-da!"

Flying

This is my family's favorite trick.

What You Need

* ❋ An adult
* ❋ A child

1. The adult lies down with his back on the floor.
2. The adult needs to bend his knees and lift his feet.
3. The child stands in front of the adult with her stomach close to the bottoms of the adult's feet.
4. The child holds the adult's hands, so her arms are stretched out horizontally.
5. On the count of three the adult lifts the child up with his feet, using his clasped hands to help balance the child.
6. While the child is balanced in the air the adult sings this circus song:

   She floats through the air with the greatest of ease.
   My little (child's name) on the flying trapeze.
   Her movements are graceful, all the crowd she does please.
   My heart she has stolen away.

On the last word of the song, the adult sets the child back on her feet.

> Wilbur and Orville Wright were two brothers who invented the airplane in the early 1900s. Before that they worked in a bike shop, where they sold and repaired bicycles.

Circus Treats

The circus is even more fun with special treats. Here are some treats the family can make together.

Animal Cracker Cars

When the circus comes to town, the animals ride in fun train cars. These train cars look fun and taste delicious!

What You Need

* Graham crackers
* Animal crackers
* Tube of icing
* Round gummy candies (the kind with a hole in the center)

1. Place a graham cracker on a table top and place one or two animal crackers on top of the graham cracker, in the center.

2. Use the tube of icing to decorate the top of the graham cracker like a circus car. Then draw vertical lines down the graham cracker and on top of the animal cracker, to make it look like the animal cracker is behind bars on the circus car.

3. Place a little bit of icing on the bottom left and bottom right of each graham cracker. Then place a candy on each bit of icing for the wheels of the car.

The Ringling brothers bought a circus show from P. T. Barnum in 1907. P. T. Barnum called the circus "The Greatest Show on Earth!"

Clown Cupcakes

Here's a delicious way to clown around with cupcakes.

What You Need

* Cupcake mix, your favorite flavor (plus the ingredients called for on the package)
* White frosting
* Ice cream cones with pointy tips
* Brightly colored candies
* Tube of icing, any bright color
* A grown-up to assist

1. Make and bake the cupcakes according to the package directions.

2. After the cupcakes have cooled, frost them with the white frosting.

3. Place an ice cream cone upside down on the side of the cupcake and only covering two-thirds of it so you have room to make a candy face. The cone is the clown's hat.

4. Use the candies to make the clown's eyes, nose, and mouth. Press these firmly into the white frosting to get them to stick.

5. Make a clown costume collar around the edges of the cupcake using the tube of icing.

Tightrope Acts and Other Pantomimes

Pantomime is acting without talking and with pretend objects. Circus clowns often use pantomime in their comedy routines. Try pantomiming your very own tightrope act.

Start at one end of the room and imagine that you are walking across a tightrope. Create an imaginary rope in your mind and never step off it. Pretend that you lose your balance at one point, then recover, then lose your balance again. You will add more drama to your routine if you prolong these recovery attempts. Try doing some tricks on the tightrope such as jumping, walking backward, and turning around. When you reach the other end of the room, jump off the imaginary tightrope and say "Ta-da!"

Circuses started in ancient Rome where great athletes would perform athletic feats. Animals were featured in the first circuses. There were chariot races, too.

Here are some other circus pantomimes you can act out:

✳ Pretend that you are holding a big helium balloon that is lifting you off the ground.

✳ Pretend that you have to pull and push a large box onto a pretend stage.

✳ Pretend that you are on slippery ice and it is very hard to walk.

✳ Pretend that you are a windup toy.

Sideshow Posters

A circus sideshow often features weird and amazing creatures, some real and some not so real. In this activity you can make all kinds of crazy characters for your own circus sideshow.

What You Need

* ❋ Magazines
* ❋ Scissors
* ❋ Paper to mount your creatures on (any size)
* ❋ Glue
* ❋ Markers
* ❋ Long sticks such as straight tree branches, broom handles, or yardsticks
* ❋ A grown-up to assist

1. Cut out pictures of people and animals from magazines using the scissors.
2. Cut these pictures into body parts such as head, body, and feet.
3. Mix and match the pictures of body parts to create unusual creatures, and glue them together on your paper.
4. Make up a name for your creature and write it on the paper.
5. Glue the paper onto the top of the stick. (You'll use this later in your parade.)

Tom Thumb was the circus name of Charles Stratton, who was a dwarf. He toured with P. T. Barnum during the early years of Barnum's circus show.

Here are some freaky examples you can try.

* ❋ Name: Ed/Edna, The Incredible Half Man/Half Woman!
  Find a picture of a man and one of a woman and cut each in half, right down the center of the picture. Glue the left side of the man to the right side of the woman. (Of course, you'll need pictures about the same size for this to work really well.)

* ❋ Name: Babyony, The Amazing Half Baby/Half Pony!
  Cut out the top half of a baby and the bottom half of a horse, and glue them together.

* ❋ Name: Rackelebot!
  Cut out the head of a raccoon, the body of an elephant, and the legs of a robot. Glue them together to make Rackelebot.

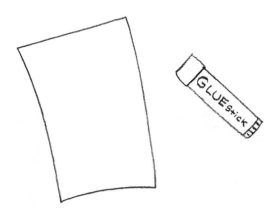

Clown Faces

Did you know that every professional clown has a unique clown face? It's true. A professional clown must register his or her clown face design with the Department of Clown Registry at Clowns International so that no other clown can have the same one. This tradition grew out of an unwritten law in the clown community that no one should copy the clown face of another. With that in mind, create your own original clown face design. Work together as a family to help incorporate each person's personality into his or her design.

> The registered clown faces are painted on eggs and preserved, many in museums.

What You Need

* Paper
* Markers or crayons
* Face paints, available at costume shops and many school supply stores

1. Begin by creating a clown face on paper with markers or crayons. Draw a big circle on the paper to represent your face and another one inside that is nearly as large. This second circle will be the area in which you draw your clown face.

2. Think of colors and shapes you like. Create eyes, a nose, and a mouth for your clown based on these ideas. Be creative! You can make one eye in the shape of a star and the other a bull's-eye. You can have a blue mouth with orange trim—anything you like!

3. Add a hat and collar to finish your design.

4. Using the face paints, draw another person's clown face on them. Then have that person paint your design on your face. Or the family can line up in front of a mirror and each family member can paint his or her own face.

Once you've created your clown face, make a clown costume. Here are some ideas:

* Put on a button-up shirt or sport coat that is way too big for you (roll up the sleeves).
* Find and put on the ugliest tie (or scarf) you can find.
* Grab the silliest hat around.

> Did you know that you could go to clown college? It's a school where actors go to learn how to be circus clowns. You can also go to Clown Camp and Clown School. More details are at www.clownevents.com.

Parade!

Now it's time for a circus parade. Parades were traditionally used by circuses to let people know that the circus was in town. Carry the flags you make in the Make Flags activity (see page 14) or the posters you created in Sideshow Posters. Use household items to make musical instruments such as an upside-down pot and a spoon for a drum, or two pot lids for cymbals. Maybe play some music and march to a beat. If it's nice outside, parade around your neighborhood. If not, just parade through your home. Here are two songs you can sing while you march in your parade:

Going to the Circus Marching Song
This is a call-and-response song that includes a lot of action.

Leader: *I'm going to the circus!*
Others: *I'm going to the circus!*
Leader: *Where I perform!*
Others: *Where I perform!*
Leader: *I've got my friends . . .*
Others: *I've got my friends . . .*
Leader: *Right by my side.*
Others: *Right by my side.*
Leader: *Oooh, train tracks.*
Others: *Oooh, train tracks.*
Leader: *Can't fly over them.*
Others: *Can't fly over them.*
Leader: *Can't go under them.*
Others: *Can't go under them.*
Leader: *Can't go around them.*
Others: *Can't go around them.*
Leader: *Gotta go across them.*
Others: *Gotta go across them.*
(Make chuga chuga, choo choo sounds as you pretend to cross the tracks.)
Leader: *I'm going to the circus!*
Others: *I'm going to the circus!*

Leader: *Where I perform!*
Others: *Where I perform!*
Leader: *I've got my friends . . .*
Others: *I've got my friends . . .*
Leader: *Right by my side.*
Others: *Right by my side.*
Leader: *Oooh, a hill.*
Others: *Oooh, a hill.*
Leader: *Can't go through it.*
Others: *Can't go through it.*
Leader: *Can't go under it.*
Others: *Can't go under it.*
Leader: *Can't go around it.*
Others: *Can't go around it.*
Leader: *Gotta go over it.*
Others: *Gotta go over it.*
(Make panting sounds as if you are climbing over a big hill.)
Leader: *I'm going to the circus!*
Others: *I'm going to the circus!*
Leader: *Where I perform!*
Others: *Where I perform!*

Leader: *I've got my friends . . .*
Others: *I've got my friends . . .*
Leader: *Right by my side.*
Others: *Right by my side.*
Leader: *Oooh, a river!*
Others: *Oooh, a river!*
Leader: *Can't go over it.*
Others: *Can't go over it.*
Leader: *Can't go under it.*
Others: *Can't go under it.*
Leader: *Can't go around it.*
Others: *Can't go around it.*
Leader: *Gotta go through it.*
Others: *Gotta go through it.*
(Make swishy water sounds as you pretend to swim across the river.)
Leader: *Now I'm at the circus so let's have fun!*
Others: *Now I'm at the circus so let's have fun!*

The Clowns Go Marching Song

Change the song "When Johnny Comes Marching Home" (you might know this as "The Ants Go Marching" instead) to when "The Clowns Go Marching" and sing along with your parade march.

The clowns go marching one by one hurrah, hurrah (Repeat)
The clowns go marching one by one, the little one stops to have some fun
And they all go marching down to the train, to get out of the rain

The clowns go marching two by two hurrah, hurrah (Repeat)
The clowns go marching two by two, the little one stops to tie his shoe
And they all go marching down to the train, to get out of the rain

The clowns go marching three by three hurrah, hurrah (Repeat)
The clowns go marching three by three, the little one stops to act silly
And they all go marching down to the train, to get out of the rain

The clowns go marching four by four hurrah, hurrah (Repeat)
The clowns go marching four by four, the little one stops to fall on the floor
And they all go marching down to the train, to get out of the rain

The clowns go marching five by five hurrah, hurrah (Repeat)
The clowns go marching five by five, the little one stops to scratch his hives
And they all go marching down to the train, to get out of the rain

The clowns go marching six by six hurrah, hurrah (Repeat)
The clowns go marching six by six, the little one stops to pick up sticks
And they all go marching down to the train, to get out of the rain

The clowns go marching seven by seven hurrah, hurrah (Repeat)
The clowns go marching seven by seven, the little one stops to look up at heaven
And they all go marching down to the train, to get out of the rain

The clowns go marching eight by eight hurrah, hurrah (Repeat)
The clowns go marching eight by eight, the little one stops to shut the gate
And they all go marching down to the train, to get out of the rain

The clowns go marching nine by nine hurrah, hurrah (Repeat)
The clowns go marching nine by nine, the little one stops to drink some wine
And they all go marching down to the train, to get out of the rain

The clowns go marching ten by ten hurrah, hurrah (Repeat)
The clowns go marching ten by ten, the little one stops to say, "The end"
And they all go marching down to the train, to get out of the rain.

Animal Trainers

Here's a fun game to play that involves pretending.

One family member is the trainer; everyone else is an animal. It's the trainer's job to get the animals to do tricks.

Here are some animal suggestions:

* Lion
* Elephant
* Seal
* Flea
* Penguin
* Dog
* Horse

Here are some trick suggestions:

* Jump through a hoop. A hula hoop works great.
* Roll over.
* Do an obstacle course. Set up pillows to jump on, chairs to walk around, and tables to crawl under.
* Do a dance.
* Do a wave. Line up all the animals and have them go down the line waving their arms one at a time.

Make Flags

You can make flags to wave as you march along in your circus parade.

What You Need

* Construction paper
* Scissors
* Markers
* Magazines
* Tape
* Long sticks such as straight tree branches, broom handles, or yardsticks
* A grown-up to assist

1. Using the scissors, cut a piece of construction paper into a long triangle.
2. Decorate it with the markers by coloring it brightly with various shapes.
3. Look through the magazines for pictures of animals. Cut these out and tape them onto the decorated paper.
4. Once you've decorated both sides of the paper, tape it to the top of your stick to make a flag. Now you're ready for the parade.

Poetry Slam Night

Dim the lights, get out those bongo drums, put on your love beads, and get ready for Poetry Slam Night! You don't have to be an award-winning poet to enjoy a poetry slam. The activities here are foolproof ways to create poems with your family.

Poetry is a great way to express yourself and to hear how others in your family express themselves. You might be a poet, and not even know it! Even if you've never thought of yourself as a poet before, you may be surprised at how, with a little help from some of these exercises, poetry can flow from you without too much effort.

For centuries poetry has been a beautiful way for people of all ages to convey their feelings and experiences. And remember, families that rhyme together have a good time together!

Bongo Jam

What You Need

* Book of poetry or nursery rhymes
* Things to drum on (a box, a pot lid, or anything you can drum on with your hands)

1. One person selects a poem. Everyone else selects a homemade drum.

2. As one person reads the poem out loud, everyone else keeps time with the drums. The drums should beat slowly and quietly enough so the reader can be heard above the sound.

3. The reader pauses after every line; this is a time for the drummers to beat more strongly and loudly.

4. When the drums resume a softer sound, the reader continues with the next line of poetry.

If you don't want to beat a drum, then snap your fingers to the same beat as the drummers.

You can do this activity with poems from a book or poems that you know by heart. Don't think you know any? Think again. Nursery rhymes are great poems! You can also use song lyrics. Speak the lyrics instead of singing them, for a poetic creation. No matter how silly they are, try saying them as seriously as you can, with dramatic pauses for the drums. Exaggerate the words and have fun with it. Here's an example:

Reader: *The itsy bitsy spider went up the waterspout!*
　　　　(Drums and snaps)
Reader: *Down came the rain and washed the spider out!*
　　　　(Drums and snaps)
Reader: *Up came the sun and dried up all the rain.*
　　　　(Drums and snaps)
Reader: *And the itsy bitsy spider went up the spout again!*
　　　　(Drums and snaps)

Sunglasses

Cool poets wear sunglasses, even in a dark club hosting a poetry slam. Here's how to make some cool poet sunglasses of your own.

What You Need

* Construction paper
* Scissors
* Colored cellophane paper
* Glue or tape
* Markers or crayons
* A grown-up to assist

1. Cut out the construction paper in the shape of sunglasses.

2. Glue or tape cellophane paper over the eyeholes.

3. Use the markers or crayons to decorate your glasses in groovy ways, with peace symbols, flowers, or words that might appear in your poems.

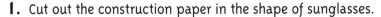

Groovy and *outta sight* were slang words used in the 1960s. See if your parents can help you think of more hip words to say while you wear your cool sunglasses.

Rhyme Time

This is a fast-paced game that requires quick thinking.

1. Sit in a circle. One player begins by saying any word.

2. The player on the left of the first person has to say a word that rhymes with the first word.

3. The game continues around the circle until someone cannot think of a rhyming word that has not been said. Then that player is out, and the next player starts a new round with a new word.

Here are some ideas for words:

* Pie
* Clam
* Star
* Ring
* Can
* Pot
* Berry

* Teen
* Hill
* Stick
* Day
* Hair
* Me
* Blue

Favorite Poems

Each family member should choose a favorite poem. You can look in the library for a book of poems, or look for poems in books you already own. For example, Lewis Carroll wrote many poems, and you can find quite a few of them in his book Alice in Wonderland. *Here is one of my favorite poems by Carroll from* Through the Looking Glass.

Jabberwocky

'Twas brillig, and the slithy toves
Did gyre and gimble in the wabe;
All mimsy were the borogoves,
And the mome raths outgrabe.

"Beware the Jabberwock, my son!
The jaws that bite, the claws that catch!
Beware the Jubjub bird, and shun
The frumious Bandersnatch!"

He took his vorpal sword in hand:
Long time the manxome foe he sought—
So rested he by the Tumtum tree,
And stood awhile in thought.

And as in uffish thought he stood,
The Jabberwock, with eyes of flame,
Came whiffling through the tulgey wood,
And burbled as it came!

One, two! One, two! And through and
  through
The vorpal blade went snicker-snack!
He left it dead, and with its head
He went galumphing back.

"And hast thou slain the Jabberwock?
Come to my arms, my beamish boy!
O frabjous day! Callooh! Callay!"
He chortled in his joy.

'Twas brillig, and the slithy toves
Did gyre and gimble in the wabe;
All mimsy were the borogoves,
And the mome raths outgrabe.

Take turns reading or reciting your favorite poem. Tell everyone why it is your favorite. Listen courteously while others read their poems, just as you want them to be courteous when you read yours.

While someone is reading a poem, everyone else should close their eyes and listen. See what images come to mind as you listen to the poem. After the poem is finished, share the images you saw with others in your family. Were they the same? Similar? Different? If you read "Jabberwocky," you might draw pictures of what you think the Jabberwock looks like.

> William Shakespeare wrote 154 sonnets in his lifetime. A sonnet is a rhyming poem with 14 lines.

Letter Poems

This poetry word game also makes a great travel game when you select a word from a billboard to create your traveling poem.

1. Choose a word to be the focus of your poem. It can be the name of a family member, a favorite thing, or a word or image from a billboard.

2. Slowly spell the word. After you say each letter in the word, say something that starts with that letter that reminds you of your word.

3. Try forming phrases from each word and then rhyming the lines.

Here's one example:

Gerda (the name of a close friend)

G is for Giddy, as happy as can be.
E is for Excellent, which is both you and me.
R is for Roses, our favorite flower.
D is for Dandelions, which are nice for about an hour.
And A is for Always as in let's always be friends!

And here's another example:

Mother

M is for the marvelous, magnificent mother have we.
O is for outstanding, all others would agree.
T is for terrific; yes, she is the very best.
H is for her helping hands, and giving us great happiness.
E is for eating; our mom's an excellent cook.
R is for responsible, for giving us great books.

Community Poems

Create poems that include contributions from every family member. That's why these are called community poems—everyone helps.

What You Need

❋ Paper

❋ Pens or pencils

1. Write down the first line of a poem. Make sure the last word isn't too difficult to rhyme.

2. Pass the paper to another family member. That person will write the second line of the poem. The last word in the second line should rhyme with the last word in the first line.

3. Pass the paper to the next family member so that person can write the third line.

4. Pass it one last time for another line to be added by a fourth person. This person gets to read the poem out loud.

Here's an example:

> Sister writes: I see a rainbow in the sky.
> Dad writes: I see a bird go flying by.
> Mom writes: I sometimes wish I could fly, too,
> Brother writes: So I could fly into the zoo.

You can make all the lines rhyme or every two lines rhyme.

If you are not sure how to start your poem, think of the words to songs or nursery rhymes, and change them a bit. Here's an example:

> *Mary had a little dog.*
> *Its collar was blue as the sea.*
> *And every time that Mary walked him,*
> *He ran around a tree.*

"A Visit from St. Nicholas" is a poem that begins with *"T'was the night before Christmas . . ."* It was written by Clement Clark Moore as a Christmas gift for his children.

Here's a famous standard poem:

> *Roses are red,*
> *Violets are blue.*
> *Sugar is sweet,*
> *And so are you.*

You can use "Roses are red" as the basis for your community poem. Here's an example of how that might work:

> *Roses smell nice,*
> *Skunks smell real bad.*
> *This poem is silly,*
> *Just like my dad!*

You can also use this game to write limericks. *Limericks* are five-line poems where the first, second, and fifth lines rhyme and the third and fourth lines rhyme. The third and fourth lines are also shorter than the others. Here's an example of a limerick:

> *There once was a brother named Marty*
> *Who thought that today was his party.*
> *He put on a tie*
> *And started to cry*
> *Because he realized he was tardy.*

See if you can create a limerick for every member of your family.

You Are Old, Father William

Here is a fun poem to read out loud together. Lewis Carroll wrote it about a young person who asks too many questions.

Younger person:

"You are old, Father William," the young man said,
"And your hair has become very white;
And yet you incessantly stand on your head—
"Do you think, at your age, it is right?"

Older person (standing on his head, if he can!):

"In my youth," father William replied to his son,
"I feared it would injure the brain;
But, now that I'm perfectly sure I have none,
Why, I do it again and again."

Younger person:

"You are old," said the youth, "as I mentioned before,
And have grown most uncommonly fat;
Yet you turned a back-somersault in at the door—
Pray what is the meaning of that?"

Older person (showing his muscles):

"In my youth," said the sage as he shook his grey locks,
"I kept all my limbs very supple
By the use of this ointment—one shilling the box—
Allow me to sell you a couple."

Younger person:

"You are old," said the youth, "and your jaws are too weak
For anything tougher than suet;
Yet you finished the goose, with the bones and the beak—
Pray how did you manage to do it?"

Older person (while exercising jaw):

"In my youth," said his father, "I took to the law,
And argued each case with my wife;
And the muscular strength, which it gave to my jaw,
Has lasted the rest of my life."

Younger person:

"You are old," said the youth, "one would hardly suppose
That your eye was as steady as ever;
Yet you balanced an eel on the end of your nose—
What made you so awfully clever?"

Older person (while kicking):

"I have answered three questions and that is enough,"
Said his father; "don't give yourself airs!
Do you think I can listen all day to such stuff?
Be off, or I'll kick you down stairs!"

Lewis Carroll was inspired by a real little girl named Alice Liddell when he wrote *Alice in Wonderland*.

21

Movie Star Night

This chapter includes a lot of Hollywood movie theme activities for families to do together. While watching a movie together is a common family night activity, this chapter will give you some ideas to make your movie-watching night a unique and special event.

Here you'll find active games to play such as charades and artistic things to do such as making movie posters. Family members of all ages will enjoy pretending to be a star by giving acceptance speeches for awards they receive, starring in an original film with the help of a video camera, doing impressions of famous celebrities, and much more. You'll have so much fun with these activities that you might never get to the movie!

Acceptance Speech

Have you ever imagined what you would say if you won an Oscar? An Oscar is the award the Academy of Motion Picture Arts and Sciences gives every spring since 1929 to honor great work in film. Here's your chance to create a special award and to practice your acceptance speech.

1. Collectively decide on the name for your family's movie award. In Hollywood, the awards are called Oscars. You can name your award after a family pet, a member of the family, or perhaps a great-grandparent who liked movies.

2. After you've decided on a name for the award, present the award to a member of your family. (The award itself can be as little as a piece of candy or as big as a piece of furniture; you decide.) Awards can be given for anything. Here are a few ideas:

   * Best I-don't-want-to-go-to-bed scene
   * Best supporting actress in the kitchen
   * Best directing award for supervising yard cleanup
   * Best garage sale salesperson
   * Best whine
   * Best joke

3. The person receiving the award stands up and gives his or her acceptance speech to the rest of the family. Here's an example of how that might sound:

   Mom: For his leading role in the movie *Creature from the Messy Room* I hereby present Leo with this year's Nobby Award.

   Leo: I'd like to thank my family for their continuous support in my effort to sustain my messy room. I'd also like to thank my grandfather, Nobby, for whom this award is named. I'd like to thank my best friend, Stacey, for helping me create the mess, and to all of my games and stuffed animals for being such a great supporting cast.

Here is a list of some people you may want to thank in your speech:

   * Family
   * Friends
   * Favorite teacher
   * Hero
   * Celebrity you admire
   * Favorite pet
   * Favorite author

> Shirley Temple won a special miniature Oscar in 1935. She is still the youngest recipient of this award.

The Paparazzi

Paparazzi are photographers who follow celebrities around and take photographs of them. In this game, you get to be both the celebrity and members of the paparazzi.

1. Decide who will be the celebrity and who will be members of the paparazzi.

2. One family member (the paparazzi) points to another family member (the celebrity) and calls out an activity.

3. The celebrity then pantomimes (pretends to do) that activity while the other family members pretend to take his picture, over and over again, in various positions, sometimes getting very close and sometimes from far away.

4. The celebrity then points to another family member and calls out another activity. The new celebrity must now pantomime an activity and the previous celebrity becomes a member of the paparazzi. That player pretends to do a new activity, while everyone else takes his picture. Continue the game until everyone has had a chance to pantomime a couple of activities before the paparazzi.

Here's an example of how to play:

❋ Sherita points to her mom, Jackie, and commands, "Brush your teeth!"

❋ Jackie pretends to brush her teeth while Sherita and her dad, Howie, pretend to take her picture, saying, "Click, click, click . . ."

❋ Jackie points to Howie and says, "Wash the car!"

❋ Howie pretends to wash the car while Sherita and Jackie take his picture.

❋ Howie points to Sherita and says, "Eat a peach!"

❋ Sherita pretends to eat a peach, while Howie and Jackie take her picture.

If you have a digital camera, you can take actual pictures of each other doing the activities, then look at them together.

Autographs

Movie stars are always asked for autographs, but you can collect autographs from a lot of not-so-famous people, too. Create a family autograph book to treasure forever. You can begin this book by collecting autographs from all of your family members. And you can add to your book by collecting autographs of guests who visit your home.

What You Need

❋ Paper

❋ Stapler

❋ Markers, crayons, or color pens

❋ Pens

1. Stack the sheets of paper together and fold them in half vertically to create a book.

2. Staple the pages together along the folded edge.

3. Decorate the outside of your autograph book using the markers or crayons.

4. Write the words "The _____ (your family name here) Autograph Book" on the cover.

5. Add headings at the top of the pages of your autograph book. Here are some examples:

   ❋ Autographs of people related to me

   ❋ Autographs of people who live on my block

   ❋ Autographs of right-handed people using their left hand

   ❋ Autographs of left-handed people writing with their right hand

   ❋ Autographs of people who can write backward

   ❋ Autographs in different languages

> Movie theaters sell more popcorn at scary movies than at any other kind of movies.

   ❋ Autographs of people who write neatly

   ❋ Autographs of people who write very messily

   ❋ Autographs of people who like to watch *Sesame Street*

   ❋ Autographs of people who can name all seven dwarfs

   ❋ Autographs of people who like broccoli

   ❋ Autographs of people who have flown on an airplane

   ❋ Autographs of musicians (please include what instrument you play)

6. Pass your book around and have family members sign their autograph on all the pages that apply to them.

7. Place the book by your front door and ask all the guests who come to your home to sign it.

You can review this book periodically with your family to learn new things about your friends and extended family.

Movie Title Charades

Charades is a game where players try to guess a word or phrase from the actions of another player who doesn't use any words. Here is a list of movie titles that are fun for any family member to act out. You can use one of these, or come up with your own.

* Babe
* Baby Geniuses
* Beauty and the Beast
* Cats and Dogs
* Chicken Run
* Fiddler on the Roof
* Finding Nemo
* Holes
* Ice Age
* The Jungle Book
* Kangaroo Jack
* The Land Before Time
* The Lion King

* The Little Mermaid
* Mouse Hunt
* The Princess Diaries
* Treasure Planet
* The Secret Garden
* Singin' in the Rain
* Snow Dogs
* Spy Kids
* Star Wars
* Toy Story
* The Wild Thornberrys
* Willy Wonka and the Chocolate Factory

1. The player who acts out the title should first indicate how many words are in the movie title by holding up the correct number of fingers.

2. Next, decide the easiest word to act out. Let the other players know which word you are acting out by holding up that number of fingers.

3. For small words like *the*, *and*, and *in*, you can make a small symbol with your fingers. The other players will know to start guessing small words until they have said the correct one.

4. Nod your head to indicate when a player has guessed a word correctly.

On other family nights you can play different kids of charades. Try book title charades, song charades, or even big events in your family's history.

Video Fun

If you have a video camera, your family can make movies together. Here are some ideas for films:

✳ Do tricks like turning into each other. Film one family member standing up still. Then stop filming and have another family member stand in the exact place using the same posture. Start filming again. In the movie, it will look like the first family member turned into the second. To make it even funnier, film a stuffed animal in the same place after the second family member. It will look like she just turned into a stuffed animal! You can say magic words on the film to add to the effect.

✳ Choose a favorite short story or book and select a chapter or section to turn into a movie. Select specific points in the book that are active and write dialogue between the characters. Dress up like the characters in the scene and film it.

✳ Film your pet or a baby doing things, while someone (off camera) talks for them. For example, while your cat is eating, a voice can say, "Cat food again? Gee, maybe if I close my eyes it will turn into tuna. Nope, didn't work. Oh well. I guess I'll have to shed all over the furniture until they get the hint."

Dubbing

Is there a movie that your family has watched so many times you practically know it by heart? Why not see if you really do?

1. Turn on your favorite movie and begin watching.
2. Figure out who will speak for which character in the film.
3. Mute the sound or turn the volume way down.
4. Begin speaking for your character when he or she appears on-screen. You can try to talk exactly like the character, or you can make up funny things the character might say.

You may not want to do this for an entire movie, but there are a number of famous movie scenes that work well for this game. Here are a few suggestions:

✳ The *Wizard of Oz* scene in which Dorothy first meets the munchkins

✳ The *Cinderella* scene in which everyone tries on the shoe

✳ The *Peter Pan* scene in which Wendy, John, and Michael learn to fly

✳ The *Snow White and the Seven Dwarfs* scene in which Snow White eats the poison apple

> Judy Garland was 16 years old when she played Dorothy in *The Wizard of Oz*.

Movie Posters

Every movie has a movie poster to advertise it. Movie posters for some older movies have become famous and collectible. Create your own original movie poster to collect in your home.

What You Need

* White paper, unlined
* Pencil
* Construction paper
* Markers or crayons
* Family photographs (optional)
* Scissors (if using photographs)
* Glue (if using photographs)
* A grown-up to assist

1. Think up a story line for a movie starring your family members, or imagine your family in a famous movie or story.

2. Select the important parts of the story for your poster.

3. Use the unlined paper and pencil to make a rough sketch of your poster. Decide which images work and where to place them on the final poster. Sketching out your poster first will help you create the most dynamic and appealing poster possible.

4. Create a name for your movie production company. You could use your family's name, such as Andrews Pictures, or you can use your initials and call it JRA Pictures, for example. The name of the production company goes at the top of the movie poster.

5. In big letters, list the names of the stars. You could use the real names of people in your family, such as "Josh Andrews and Suzie Andrews" or "Roberto Lopez as Luis Rodriguez" or use your movie star name. Here's how you can create your movie star name:

   Take your middle name as your first name.
   Your last name is the street you live on.

   For example if your middle name is Robert and you live on Leamington Avenue, your movie star name is Robert Leamington.

If you want your parents to have different last names, use the streets they grew up on for their last names.

6. Next, in even bigger letters, write the name of the movie. You can make it up or use a famous movie or story title. Or you could combine both ideas. Your family movie could include part of a famous title and part of a real thing about your family. For example, for the title *The Wizard of Oz*, change the word Oz to be the town you live in, such as "The Wizard of Chicago." Or in *Snow White and the Seven Dwarfs*, change the word Dwarfs to your last name, such as "Snow White and the Seven Lopeses," or change it to your parent's occupation, "Snow White and the Seven Lawyers."

7. Draw a picture or use photographs of your family (remember to ask before using these) that look as if they are a scene from a movie.

Here's a sample of the text for your movie poster:

JRA Pictures presents
Robert Leamington
Jay Fortuna
Barbara Irving
in
Lady and the Champs

King Kong was the first movie to have a sequel. It was called *Son of Kong*.

Who Am I?

Impressions are when you try to sound like another person. Some famous comedians are known for their impressions or impersonations of famous people. Here's your chance to do impressions of your favorite actors or characters from the movies. See if other family members can guess who you are impersonating. Here are some suggestions of lines you can say for your impression:

✳ "Toto, I've got a feeling we're not in Kansas anymore." Dorothy from *The Wizard of Oz*

✳ "You stole fizzy lifting drink!" Willy Wonka from *Willy Wonka and the Chocolate Factory*

✳ "To infinity, and beyond!" Buzz Lightyear from *Toy Story*

✳ "Spit, spot!" Mary Poppins from *Mary Poppins*

✳ "I got a rock." Charlie Brown from *It's the Great Pumpkin, Charlie Brown*

✳ "Luke, I am your father." Darth Vader from *Star Wars: Episode V—The Empire Strikes Back*

✳ "It came without presents!" The Grinch from *How the Grinch Stole Christmas*

✳ "All I want is . . . your voice." Ursula from *The Little Mermaid*

✳ "All you need is faith and trust, and a little bit of pixie dust." Peter Pan from *Peter Pan*

✳ "I want to be a dentist." Herbie the Elf from *Rudolph the Red-Nosed Reindeer*

✳ "T.T.F.N. Ta-ta for now!" Tigger from *Winnie the Pooh*

✳ "Curiouser and curiouser." Alice from *Alice in Wonderland*

✳ "Look at me and my bad self." Emperor Kusco from *The Emperor's New Groove*

Ninety-eight percent of all U.S. households own at least one television set; 64 percent have two or more sets. Before television, families sang songs, told stories, and danced. This is how many professional entertainers developed their skills in the past.

✳ "Happy Birthday!" Frosty the Snowman from *Frosty the Snowman*

✳ "E.T. phone home." from *E.T. the Extra Terrestrial*

✳ "Mirror, mirror on the wall, who's the fairest one of all?" The queen from *Snow White and the Seven Dwarfs*

Another fun twist on the game is to do impressions of each other. Don't make fun of other family members, but try to do as close an impression as you can.

"To infinity, and beyond!"

Giggle Night

You'll get a great response when you announce to your family that tonight is Giggle Night!

It is often said that laughter is the best medicine. Family members can forget their problems and worries by taking time for something extremely important: laughing together!

Young children love to laugh and giggle, and older ones—even teenagers who may be reluctant at first—can't help but giggle when playing with food to make funny faces, playing word tricks, making up silly stories without even knowing it, and more. When you discover something that makes someone in your family giggle, remember it, and break it out on Giggle Night!

Funny Food Faces

In this activity you use food to create funny faces.

A man named John Montagu, who was actually the Earl of Sandwich, invented the sandwich.

What You Need

* Toothpicks
* Food in a variety of shapes, such as grapes, bananas, apples, raisins, and pickles
* Paper plates

1. Make an eye with an eyeball by using a toothpick to stick a raisin onto a grape. Make another eyeball, and put both onto the paper plate.
2. Peel a banana. Use the peel for hair and the banana for a mouth.
3. Place a pickle in the middle of the plate to be a nose. Be creative—use different foods for different parts of the face.
4. Look at each other's funny faces. Make up names for each face before you eat them.

Joke Time

Family members of all ages tell jokes. One of the best ways to remember someone is to remember how they used to tell a certain joke. Grandparents, parents, and kids of all ages have jokes to tell, so everyone can spend some time laughing together.

Take turns telling jokes. Even if everyone has heard the joke before, tell it anyway. Or see if you can make up a new way to tell it. Here's an example:

Knock, knock.
Who's there?
Interrupting cow.
Interrupting cow wh—?
(interrupting) Moo!

Can you think of more interrupting animals? How about an interrupting witch? An interrupting baby? Or an interrupting librarian ("Shh!")? My family's favorite is the interrupting crazy head!

The cow pictured on Elmer's Glue is named Elsie. She is the mate of Elmer, the steer that the glue is named after.

Trick Time

It's fun to play tricks on each other, and these good-hearted tricks will make the entire family giggle. One person leads the rest of the family in this counting game. The leader starts the pattern and asks each additional family member to follow the pattern:

> You say, "I one the purple cow."
> They say, "I two the purple cow."
> You say, "I three the purple cow."
> They say, "I four the purple cow."
> You say, "I five the purple cow."
> They say, "I six the purple cow."
> You say, "I seven the purple cow."
> They say, "I eight the purple cow."
> You say, "You ate a purple cow?!?!"

See what other silly things you can say they ate.

Here's another variation: tell a family member you're going to teach them a new language, and ask them to repeat after you:

> Oh wah
> Tah goo
> Siam

Then have them say it all together. It will sound like this: Oh, what a goose I am!

> The spur-winged goose is one of the fastest birds in the world. It can fly up to 88 miles per hour!

Laughs

Laughter is contagious. When one person starts laughing, others usually start, too—they can't help it.

Take turns making up funny laughs. See how many you can come up with and how many other members of your family can create. No need to declare a winner here because everyone wins when there's laughter. Here are some suggestions for characters that have a distinctive laugh:

* Witch
* Santa
* The Count from *Sesame Street*
* Nasal laugh (through your nose)
* Silent laugh
* Gasping laugh
* Giggle
* Proper laugh
* Laughter you're trying to hold in, but can't
* Snorting laugh
* High-pitched laugh
* Loud and boisterous laugh

> Kids laugh more than adults! A six-year-old laughs an average of 300 times a day, while an adult only laughs about 15 times a day. Lighten up, parents!

Funny Fill-Ins for the Family

All families have stories that they tell. These are the stories that you've heard over and over again. This activity is about how you can retell these stories with new twists by turning them into fill-in stories.

What You Need

❋ Paper

❋ Pencil

1. Write out a story about your family. It can be true or made up. Then take out some of the key words of the story and replace them with blanks.

2. Ask other family members to fill in those blanks by telling you a noun, adjective, verb, color, place, or whatever it is you need in your story. But don't let them read or hear the story.

3. After all the blanks have been filled in, read the story out loud.

Here's an example using a true story from my family:

The Beautiful Day Michaela Was Born

On the day Michaela was born, I went to the grocery store and bought all sorts of healthy foods. When I got home, I found out that it was time to go to the hospital.

When I arrived at the hospital, Grandpa was already there waiting for me.

The staff took me up to my room in a wheelchair, and prepared me for my baby's delivery.

As soon as Michaela was born, a nurse laid her on my chest. She was so beautiful.

Now here's the same story with a funny fill-in version:

The _____ (adjective) Day Michaela Was Born

On the day Michaela was born, I went to _____ (place) and bought all sorts of _____ (adjective) _____ (plural noun).

When I got home, I found out that it was time to go to the _____ (place).

When I arrived at the hospital, _____ (person) was already there waiting for me.

The staff took me up to my room in a _____ (mode of transportation), and prepared me for my baby's delivery.

As soon as Michaela was born, a nurse laid her on my _____ (body part). She was so _____ (adjective).

Here's an example of how it came out with the crazy fill-in version:

The Crazy Day Michaela Was Born

On the day Michaela was born, I went to Disney World and bought all sorts of lumpy kittens. When I got home, I found out that it was time to go to the toy store.

When I arrived at the hospital, Bugs Bunny was already there waiting for me.

The staff took me up to my room in a motorcycle, and prepared me for my baby's delivery.

As soon as Michaela was born, a nurse laid her on my elbow. She was so orange.

Sticky Icky Night

It's fun to get sticky and icky. What parents find gross, kids often find cool. So tell your parents to relax and prepare to get sticky icky, just for one night!

These activities include testing your recall abilities, making taffy out of marshmallows, making delicious popcorn balls, and more.

Seeing-Eye Hands

Sometimes things are not as they feel. When you're in a spooky frame of mind, everyday food and items can feel like untouchables. Have extra napkins on hand for this game where each person tries to "see" with his or her hands.

> There is a creature called a sea cucumber. It lives in the ocean and looks like it is covered with warts. When attacked, it throws out sticky threads from inside its mouth.

What You Need

* Variety of foods and other items, such as peeled grapes, cooked pasta, gelatin, wet bread, peeled pickles, catsup, a wet sponge, wet toilet tissue, a hairbrush, a doll's head
* Plates
* Napkins

1. Place any number of the things listed on separate plates while everyone else is out of the room.
2. Cover each plate with a napkin.
3. Bring one member of your family into the room and have her close her eyes.
4. Guide her hand to feel a food item on one plate without opening her eyes.
5. Ask her to tell you what it feels like. Maybe you have a plate of peeled grapes. Do they feel like eyeballs? Let her open her eyes and see what the item is before moving on to the next item.

Licorice Sculptures

What You Need

* Strands of licorice, the pull-n-peel kind
* Plates

1. Pull the long pieces of the licorice apart.
2. Use them to create images on your plate. You can shape them into lines on a plate for two-dimensional art such as:

   * A funny face
   * A house
   * A heart

You can coil them and pile them on top of each other to make three-dimensional sculptures such as:

   * A basket
   * A robot
   * A flower

You can create wearable jewelry with them, such as:

   * A necklace
   * A bracelet
   * A ring

It may get a little sticky, but that's OK because it's Sticky Icky Night!

> A giraffe has a very sticky tongue. It's black and can be as long as 18 inches!

Marshmallow Pull

What You Need

* Marshmallows

1. Make sure your hands are clean!
2. Take a marshmallow and start squishing it and squeezing it between your fingers. Keep doing this until the marshmallow begins to feel and look like taffy.
3. Add more marshmallows to it until you've created a large amount of taffy.
4. Stand facing another family member. Each of you takes an end of the marshmallow taffy and pulls it away from the other. Don't pull so far that the taffy breaks. After you've pulled it back, bring the ends back together again (as if you are folding a sheet) and pull from the new ends. Continue until the taffy is at a nice, soft consistency. Enjoy it when it's done.

Cup of Mud

Would you eat a cup of mud with worms crawling out? You will if you make it like this!

What You Need

* Chocolate cookies with cream filling
* Cups
* Chocolate pudding
* Gummy worms

1. Place some pudding in a cup.
2. Crush and crumble the chocolate cookies onto the pudding.
3. Stick the gummy worms inside so they look like they are crawling out. Now eat and enjoy.

You can also make your cup of mud in a small, clean flowerpot. When you create it this way, it really looks like mud! You can even put fake flowers into the flowerpot full of mud. Place the pot on the table like a centerpiece at a party. Surprise the guests by diving into the mud with your spoon and eating it, without telling them it's really pudding.

Popcorn Balls

It's fun to make popcorn balls—if you don't mind getting your hands a bit gooey.

What You Need

* ❊ A large bowl
* ❊ Popcorn (already popped), about 6 cups
* ❊ Measuring cup
* ❊ Corn syrup
* ❊ Wax paper
* ❊ A willingness to get sticky
* ❊ A grown-up to assist

1. Put popped popcorn in a large bowl.

2. Pour 1/2 cup of corn syrup over the popcorn. Mix it up with your hands. Pour a little more corn syrup over the popcorn (if needed to make it consistently sticky), and mix it again. Continue until all popcorn is glazed with the syrup.

3. Take a large handful of the glazed popcorn. Shape it into a ball by squeezing it in your cupped hands, just as you would if you were making a snowball. Turn it around and around, squeezing gently, until it holds its shape.

4. Place it on the wax paper. Continue making popcorn balls until all of the popcorn is used.

These are ready to eat right away—nice and sticky. If you refrigerate them, they'll get nice and hard. After refrigerating, wrap them in wax paper and give them to friends.

Splash Night

It's fun to get wet and to experiment with water. Here are some great ways to do it together as a family.

For snacks on this family fun night, try foods that are heavy on the water: put food coloring into your drinking water, eat some celery (it's 90 percent water), or enjoy a slice of watermelon.

Consider wearing your bathing suit and having towels close by, so you aren't afraid to get wet. Don't worry, it's only water!

Does It Float?

This activity tests your ability to predict the future.

What You Need

* Large bucket
* Water
* Objects that can get wet

* Paper
* Pencil or pen
* A grown-up to assist

Here are some objects to try:

* Apple
* Bar of soap
* Baby food jar, full
* Baby food jar, empty

* Penny
* Small plastic toy
* Key

1. Fill a large bucket with water.
2. Have each family member search around the house for an object that can get wet.
3. Each family member takes turns presenting his or her object(s). Everyone guesses whether each object will float when placed in the bucket of water.
4. Someone keeps score by writing down everyone's name and the object to test, and then checking the appropriate box for each family member who thinks the object will float or sink. Use the table below as a model.
5. Place one object at a time in the bucket. Does it float? Who guessed correctly? If you like, you can keep track of points—one point for each correct guess.

A frog's eyes and nose are on top of its body so it can see and breathe while its body is underwater.

Name	Object	Thinks It Will Float	Thinks It Will Sink	Guessed Correctly

Paper Towel Art

This is a neat trick that turns paper towels into beautiful works of watercolor art.

What You Need

* Paper towels
* Water-based markers
* Hangers with clips

1. Each person draws a picture on a paper towel with markers.
2. Wet the paper towels. Notice how the colors soften and look more like watercolor paints.
3. Hang the paper towels to dry.
4. Once the paper towels are dry, see if you can still see the original pictures that were drawn on each of them.

Artists often paint pictures of family members. The painting known as "Whistler's Mother" is actually entitled *Arrangement in Black and Gray: The Artist's Mother*. It was painted by James McNeill Whistler.

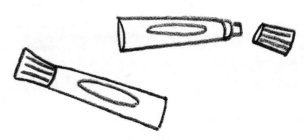

Boat Races

For this activity you can use toy boats you already have, or make your own. Here's how:

What You Need

* Small, empty plastic container (such as from cream cheese or butter)
* Clay or tape
* 6-inch long stick or a plastic straw cut down to 6 inches
* Ruler
* Scissors
* Paper
* Crayons
* Tub of water
* A grown-up to assist

Another name for a submarine is a U-boat, which stands for undersea boat.

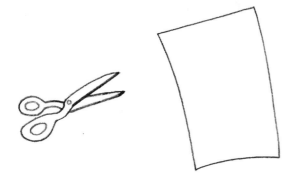

1. Place a small ball of clay in the middle of the container. If you don't have clay, then use tape to secure the stick (see step 2).

2. Push the stick or straw into the clay so that it stands up at least 4 inches above the rim of the container. If you don't have clay, then use tape to secure the stick or straw.

3. Cut a triangle out of the paper that is no larger than 2 inches across at its base.

4. Affix the triangle to the stick or straw with tape. This is your boat's sail.

5. Use crayons to color the outside of your boat (the container). You can even name your boat.

6. Fill a tub with water.

7. Each boat maker should stand on one side of the tub and lightly hold his or her boat. Simultaneously release the boats, with each player moving his or her sail by blowing on it—no hands are used once the boats are released. If there isn't enough room for everyone to line up, then hold relays with two players at once. Winners of each race should race the other winners until there is an overall winner. The losers of each race should race each other, too.

Not-So-Soaking Water Fight

While water fights can be great fun, they're not usually an indoor activity. Here are ways to have water fights that will only get everything a little bit wet.

What You Need

* ❋ Squirt bottles, one for each player
* ❋ Water
* ❋ Paper
* ❋ Crayons
* ❋ Tape
* ❋ Paper and pen (if you want to keep score)

1. Fill the squirt bottles with water.
2. Create a target by drawing circles onto a piece of paper using a crayon. (Crayons won't run when they get wet.) Make the first circle small and in the center of the paper. The next circle should be at least an inch outside the first circle. Continue to draw circles with the crayon to the outer edge of the paper.
3. Tape the target to a wall. (Check with a grown-up first.) Have each family member try to squirt the target. Give points to the family member who comes closest to squirting the center of the target. If you plan to keep score over time, number each circle, with the largest number in the center of the target. Use a new target for each match.

In Finland, Donald Duck was almost banned years ago because he didn't wear pants.

Ducks

Here is a variation of the game where your family members are the targets, instead of a paper target. In this version of the game, family members walk back and forth quacking while one family member tries to squirt them. Award one point for every hit.

Drink It

Another way to play is to try to squirt water into each other's mouths. Open your mouth and see if other family members can aim their squirt bottle so that you get a drink.

Opposite Night

This is a terrible night of no fun to not share with your family—in opposite language, that is! On Opposite Night the idea is to say the opposite of everything you mean. For example, tell your family not to gather around because you don't want to spend any time with them. Here are additional fun ideas that can make your Opposite Night memorable:

* Eat dessert before dinner.
* Let the moms and dads behave like the kids, and the kids behave like moms and dads.
* See how fast you can spell Mississippi backward.
* See how fast you can say the alphabet backward.
* See how far you can get walking backward.

Now stop reading here. (Did I fool you?)

Dressing Backward

To dress for Opposite Night, here are ideas for how you can wear your clothes in an opposite way:

* Wear all of your clothes inside out.
* Wear all of your clothes backward.
* If you're a girl, dress like a boy; and if you're a boy, dress like a girl.
* If you're a grown-up, dress like a kid; and if you're a kid, dress like a grown-up.

Here are some specific suggestions to achieve these looks:

* For a girl to dress as a man, she can paint a mustache on her face. Use face paints or eyeliner to draw a mustache, beard, and sideburns, if you wish.
* A dad can use a pillowcase for a diaper to dress as a baby.
* A woman can wear a baseball hat backward and carry around a glove and baseball to dress as a boy or girl.

Australia has seasons that occur at opposite times from when they do in the United States. Therefore when it's winter here, it's summer there, and vice versa.

Pass the Sweatshirt

Wearing your clothes inside out is one option for Opposite Night. But how about turning your clothes inside out again and again while passing them along to other family members? In this activity you'll get to see how fast you can go from inside out to right side out without getting tangled up.

The term *berserk* comes from the Nordic word for bear shirt. It refers to doing battle without any armor or even a shirt on.

What You Need

* 1 sweatshirt big enough for the largest family member to wear

1. One family member begins this activity by putting the sweatshirt on with the right side out.
2. The first family member chooses another family member to go next. And he or she passes it on. How is this done? To pass the shirt on, the two family members must face each other, hold hands, and rest their heads together. A third family member then lifts the sweatshirt up over the head of the first member and pulls it down over the second family member. The first person has to pull the second person's arms through to make it work. Now the shirt is inside out on a new person.
3. Continue passing the sweatshirt on until every family member has had a turn wearing the shirt.

After you do this once, try it again and time yourselves, and then a third time. Did your time improve?

Backward Speak

Here's another way to continue the opposite theme.

What You Need

* Paper, 1 sheet for each family member
* Pen, 1 for each family member
* Adhesive tape

1. Write your name on a piece of paper. Now write your name backward.

2. Try to pronounce your backward name out loud.

3. Pass your paper to another family member and see how he or she pronounces your name spelled backward.

4. Keep passing the papers until everyone has practiced pronouncing everyone else's name.

5. Now use these names for the rest of the evening whenever you want to speak to another family member. For example, if your brother's name is Martin, call him Nitram. Tape your backward name paper to your shirt to help other family members remember it.

   Another way to read your backward writing on opposite night is with the help of a mirror. Write the letters of your name backward, from right to left on the page, and then hold the paper in front of you and reflecting in a mirror.

Once everyone has mastered backward names, try writing or speaking other words or sentences backward. Can anyone in your family understand what you mean?

Two Truths and a Lie

A lie is, of course, the opposite of the truth. In this game, see how well your family knows you, and if you can trick them by being a good liar.

Take turns saying three things about yourself. Two of them should be true things; one of them should be a lie. See if the other members of your family can guess which one is the lie. Here are some examples of things to say:

* 3 kinds of foods you like (one of them should be a food you really hate)

* 3 places in the world you'd like to visit (one of them should be a place you don't care to visit)

* 3 things you did at school today (one of them you really didn't do today)

* 3 things in your room right now (one of them is not really in your room)

Oranges to Oranges

This game is the opposite of the family card game Apples to Apples.

Choose one player to be the first judge. The judge says an adjective, such as yummy. Each of the other family members says something that is the opposite of the word, in this case yummy. Here are some examples:

* Brussels sprouts
* Liver
* Dirty socks
* Eyeballs

The judge picks which one he likes best as the opposite of yummy. The family member who used this word gets a point.

Then it's another family member's turn to be judge and pick the adjective.

Here are some adjectives that work well for this game:

* Pretty (say things that are ugly)
* Hot (say things that are cold)
* Sad (say things that are happy)
* Nice (say things that are mean)
* Little (say things that are big)

> An orange tree can bear oranges for a hundred years!

Animal Night

If your family is made up of animal lovers, this night's for you.

Humans have always been drawn to animals. We study them, we train them, and we love them. Even the youngest children will smile at a puppy or get excited when watching a monkey at the zoo. A family pet is often considered a member of the family, and even if your family has no pets, I'm sure you have stuffed animals that you love.

You might want to paint your face like an animal and eat some animal crackers on this night. You can also make centipede bread. If you have animal print clothing, wear it. Make pet rocks and play animal games to enjoy Animal Night!

Pet Rocks

With this activity you create your own pets.

What You Need

❋ Rocks

❋ Tempera paint, available at craft supply stores

❋ Paintbrushes or markers

❋ Craft glue

❋ Craft supplies such as feathers, googly eyes, pom-poms, and more

> In the wintertime a ptarmigan (TAR-mi-gan), a type of bird that lives in the far north Canadian tundra, grows feathers on its feet to make snowshoes.

1. Each family member should go outside and find a rock. As you look for a rock to paint, think about the kind of animal you'd like your rock to resemble and look for a rock in roughly the shape of that animal.

2. Once you find your rock, take it inside and wash it with warm soap and water. You can begin painting the rock as soon as it's completely dry.

3. Using either your imagination or a picture of the animal you want your rock to resemble, begin painting your rock. Paint your rock the colors of your chosen animal.

4. Once the bottom layer of paint is dry (for your rock animal's body), next add eyes, a mouth, a nose, a snout, feathers, or fur if needed.

5. Use craft glue to affix additional items to the rock including feathers, funny eyes, and more.

6. Once your animal is dry, give it a name.

You can also create a home for your animal using a small box, such as a jewelry box. Once each family member has created a pet rock, you can put them all together to create a pet rock zoo.

Doggie, Doggie

Here's a game where you solve the mystery of the stolen bone!

What You Need

❋ A bone or something you can pretend is a bone, such as a hairbrush

1. One family member leaves the room.

2. One family member takes the bone.

3. Everyone left in the room puts their hands behind their backs.

4. Everyone left in the room calls back the person who left. Call this person by barking together.

5. When the missing person returns, everyone else says, "Doggie, doggie, where's your bone? Somebody stole it from your home! Guess who! Maybe you! Maybe the monkeys from the zoo!"

6. The person who left the room selects the person who she thinks has the bone by pointing to the person. If she guesses correctly, then she gets to stay in the room and the person who had the bone leaves the room, and the game begins again. If the person who left the room doesn't guess correctly the first time, she guesses again. If by the third try she still has not guessed correctly, then she leaves the room again, the bone is switched to one of the remaining family members, and the game begins again.

7. Play until everyone has a chance to leave the room and guess.

The fastest dog is the greyhound. Evidence suggests they existed in ancient Egypt. Greyhounds can run up to 45 miles per hour. If you're interested in adopting a greyhound, check out this Web site: www.adopt-a-greyhound.org.

Centipede Bread

Here's a yummy, buggy treat.

What You Need

* ❋ 4 eggs
* ❋ 4 small bowls
* ❋ 4 spoons
* ❋ 4 colors of food coloring
* ❋ Paintbrushes
* ❋ Ready-made biscuits in a tube (found in a grocery store's refrigerated section)
* ❋ Cookie sheet
* ❋ Toothpicks
* ❋ 2 olives
* ❋ Shredded carrots
* ❋ A grown-up to assist

1. To make the "paint," separate the egg yolk from the rest of the egg while standing over the kitchen sink. To do this, gently crack the shell and open it into two parts. Catch the yolk in one half of the shell, and then pass it to the other half of the shell. The egg white will fall out of the shell and into the sink. Keep passing it back and forth like so for a few times. Once the egg white is separated out, place the egg yolk in a bowl. If you need help, ask a grown-up.

Centipedes always have an odd number of pairs of legs, ranging anywhere from 15 to 171 pairs.

2. Add a drop of one food coloring and stir. Add more drops for deeper colors.

3. Repeat this with three other egg yolks and colors in separate bowls.

4. Place the biscuits on a cookie sheet and line them up so that they look like the body of a centipede. The biscuits should be touching; squeeze them together so that they stick during baking.

5. Using paintbrushes and the paint you made, paint designs on the tops of all of the biscuits. Use as many or as few colors as you want on each biscuit. Combine colors to create even more colors.

6. Bake the biscuits as directed on the package.

7. After the biscuits cool, use toothpicks to insert carrot shreds for antennae, a smile, and legs for your centipede.

8. Use toothpicks to stick the olives onto the head biscuit for the eyes.

Camouflage

Camouflage means using color to blend in with the surroundings. Many animals do this to hide from their enemies. This is a hiding game that's fun for the entire family. All ages will enjoy hiding and seeking the animals, which are camouflaged in your home.

What You Need

* ❋ Different colors of paper

* ❋ Markers, crayons, or pens

* ❋ Scissors

* ❋ Tape

* ❋ A grown-up to assist

1. Think of an animal you would like to hide. Either choose a piece of paper that is the color of that animal, or draw the animal on white paper and color it with crayons or markers.

2. Cut the animal out of the paper.

3. Find a place in your home where things are the same color as the animal, and place your animal in plain view next to these things. For example, if your animal is a blue whale, place your cutout on a blue bedsheet. If your animal is a yellow bird, tape your cutout on a wall that is painted yellow.

4. See if the other members of your family can find the camou-flaged animals.

> How far will you go for a meal? A golden eagle will hunt in a 100-mile area to find food for its young.

> A camel's spine is straight, even though it has a hump.

Here are some Web sites with pictures of animals in the wild to inspire your drawings:

* ❋ www.thewildones.org

* ❋ www.coolanimalpictures.com

* ❋ www.animaltrek.com

You can also play this game in reverse by finding a hiding place in your home first. Then, based on the colors of that place, create an animal to be camouflaged there.

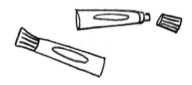

Indoor Garden Night

Whether or not you have a green thumb, you may enjoy turning your home into an indoor garden. Flowers and plants can beautify your home, and there are a lot of ways a family can work together to do just that. Seeds can be planted on one night, and the results—watching the plants grow and replanting them outdoors—can be continued for months to come.

Many people talk to their plants. Research has shown that plants actually grow better when they are talked to and taken good care of, just like a family. Plants can also be good for your health. As they breathe, they filter out some particles that can make you cough, and they give you oxygen to breathe!

Backyard in a Bottle

If you live in an apartment or someplace where you don't have a yard, then you will really appreciate learning how to create a backyard in a bottle. Even if you do have a yard, here's a garden you can enjoy in any kind of weather.

What You Need

* 2 clear plastic liter bottles
* Potting soil
* Variety of backyard seeds, including grass seed
* A grown-up to assist
* Sharp scissors or knife
* Water
* Heavy-duty tape, such as duct tape

1. Cut the top third off the plastic bottles. Recycle the discarded tops.
2. Fill half of one of the now-open bottles with potting soil.
3. Plant different seeds in the soil, including grass seeds and plant seeds.
4. Add water until the soil is damp but not soaked.
5. Turn the second now-open bottle upside down and carefully fit it over the bottle with the soil and seeds. Do this carefully, as the edges of the cut plastic will be sharp.
6. Use heavy-duty tape to tape the bottles together and make an airtight seal. The moisture will be trapped inside the bottle. After it builds up inside, it will rain down onto the soil and help the seeds grow.

Watch as the seeds germinate and grow into a bottle backyard over several weeks.

Veggie Head

The original Mr. Potato Head game came with face parts, and children supplied their own real potato. In this activity you use your own vegetables.

During Hanukkah, Jewish families make and eat potato pancakes, also known as *latkes*.

What You Need

* Pipe cleaners or Popsicle sticks
* Heavy cardstock paper
* Crayons, pencils, and markers
* Solid fruits or vegetables such as apples, melons, carrots, or potatoes
* Clear adhesive tape
* Metal paper clips
* Scissors
* A grown-up to assist

1. Select a fruit or vegetable.
2. Use pipe cleaners and Popsicle sticks to make the arms.
3. Draw face parts, such as eyes, nose, and mouth, on heavy paper and cut them out.
4. Bend a paper clip so that one tip is sticking straight out at 90 degrees from the rest of the clip.
5. Insert the straight edge of the paper clip into the place on the fruit where you want to put the eyes, nose, or mouth of your vegetable.
6. Tape the cut-out body part to the flat edge of the paper clip that remains outside the fruit or vegetable.

Trade face parts with your family members to make different faces for your veggie heads.

Egg Carton Greenhouse

Here's a way to recycle and turn your garbage into a lovely greenhouse.

What You Need

* Spoon
* Cardboard egg carton, empty
* Potting soil
* Marigold seeds
* Measuring spoons

* Clear plastic wrap
* Water
* Tape
* Scissors
* A grown-up to assist

1. Use a spoon to fill the inside of each cup of an empty egg carton with potting soil.

2. Place one marigold seed in each cup and push it gently into the soil using your finger. Cover the hole you make with soil.

3. Water the soil just enough to make the soil damp, about 1 tablespoon.

4. Tear off a piece of clear plastic wrap that is about 6 inches longer than the egg carton. Place the plastic over the cups with the soil and seeds so that some of the wrap hangs over each end of the carton. Fold the wrap down over the carton on all sides.

5. Tape the plastic tightly in place. The plastic will trap moisture in the soil so you don't have to water it again.

6. Close the lid of the carton because seeds need to germinate in the dark.

7. Place the carton in a warm spot.

8. Check the seeds every few days until you see they are sprouting—until you see tiny green leaves sticking out. Once sprouts appear, then remove the plastic.

9. Move the carton to a sunny windowsill and make sure the soil does not dry out. Not too much water either! Every day, put your finger in the soil to feel its dampness. If it feels dry, add a tablespoon of water.

10. When the plants are as tall as your index finger, carefully cut apart the cups into 12 separate cups.

11. Select a spot outside that gets full sun during the middle of the day. Plant each plant directly into a hole just as wide as the cup and just as deep as the cup. (The egg carton cup will decompose—that is, break apart—and give nutrients to the plant as it grows.) Space the plants apart by 12 inches.

Watering Cup

When watering small seeds and plants, you don't want a strong gush of water from a faucet. Instead, you want a light sprinkle. Here's a great way to create your own watering cup.

What You Need

* 2 paper cups
* Pointy tool such as a pencil or a thin knife
* Water
* A grown-up to assist

1. Use the pointy object to make eight tiny holes in the bottom of a paper cup.
2. Place a second cup (we'll call it a filler cup) inside the watering cup while it is not being used.
3. When you are ready to use your watering cup, take out the filler cup and fill it with water.
4. While holding the watering cup over the plants to be watered, slowly pour the cup filled with water into the watering cup.
5. As the water leaks out of the bottom, move the watering cup over all the plants to be watered until all the water has poured out.

   Repeat this process until the soil is evenly moist.

There's a town in Chile called Calama where it never rains. Calama is in the Atacama Desert in northern Chile, on the west side of the Andes Mountains.

Bean and Seed Art

Beans and seeds come in so many different shapes and sizes. It's fun to create pretty mosaics with them.

What You Need

* Coloring book
* Scissors
* White glue
* Paint brush or craft stick
* Variety of dry beans (pinto, lima, navy, and kidney) or seeds (sunflower or pumpkin)
* A grown-up to assist

1. Cut out a page from a coloring book that hasn't been colored.
2. Add glue to part of the picture to be colored, such as the shirt on a picture of a little boy. Use the paint brush or craft stick to spread the glue.
3. Cover the glued area with beans and seeds.
4. Add glue to another part of the picture and add more beans or seeds to your picture. Continue until the picture is completely colored with beans and seeds.

   You can either use the same bean and seed colors in a section, such as on the little boy's shirt, or you can mix and match them.

Kitchen Scraps

Watching your kitchen scraps sprout and grow can be exciting and interesting. See what happens to your kitchen scraps. Often, these scraps will re-root, and you can watch them growing under the soil through the plastic bottle.

What You Need

* ❋ 1 or more clear plastic liter bottles
* ❋ Sharp scissors or knife
* ❋ Potting soil
* ❋ Scraps of food (carrot tops with part of the carrot still attached, onions, garlic, uncooked corn on the cob, potatoes, or a pineapple top)
* ❋ Water
* ❋ A grown-up to assist

Do you recycle your newspaper? It takes 63,000 trees to make the average Sunday edition of the *New York Times*.

1. Cut the top third off one or more of the plastic bottles. Recycle the discarded tops.
2. Fill the bottle halfway with potting soil.
3. Plant the vegetables and pineapple top in different bottles, leaving only the top of the vegetable or pineapple sticking out of the soil.
4. Water just until the soil is moist. Water the soil every few days, or often enough to keep the soil moist.

Watch your kitchen scraps grow. What part begins to grow first? Do you recognize the new plant as the same thing you ate? What parts of plants do people eat?

If the plant survives and thrives, you should transplant it into a larger container for an indoor plant, or outdoors in a sunny spot so long as it is during your area's growing season. You may get a new plant that you can eat for the second time. (Note: Pineapples are tropical bromeliads and won't grow into a new tree unless you live in a tropical place. This activity will not work with most fruits such as apples, oranges, and grapes.)

Hot Potato

Here's a traditional game that works well on Indoor Garden Night.

What You Need

* 1 ball or potato
* Oven timer

1. Family members sit in a circle.
2. Someone sets the timer for a period of time, such as 20 seconds.
3. Once the timer is set, start passing the ball or potato around the circle clockwise. (Don't look at the timer—that's cheating.)
4. When the timer goes off, the person holding the potato is out. If you drop the potato as you are passing it, you are out. (This will keep a player from just throwing it as soon as it's passed to you.)
5. Reform your circle, tighter. Reset the timer for 20 seconds and continue passing the ball or potato.
6. Continue until there is only one person left—that person is the winner.

You can change the pattern of this game, too, to add to the fun. Here are some ideas:

* Reverse the direction of the ball or potato.
* Clap your hands once as the ball or potato is tossed to you.
* Close your eyes and try passing the ball or potato.

German families serve their potato salad warm.

Magic Bean

In the story "Jack and the Beanstalk," Jack traded his cow for magic beans, which grew into a giant beanstalk. Beans do grow in magical ways. Here's how you can see it happen.

What You Need

* Paper towel
* 1 or more clear plastic liter bottles
* Scissors or knife
* 1 or more dry pinto or kidney beans (not canned)
* Water
* 2 plates
* Potting soil
* A grown-up to assist

1. Place a pinto or kidney bean onto a paper towel and fold over the paper towel.
2. Dampen the paper towel with water and let it sit on the plate for a few days.
3. Check the paper towel regularly and keep it damp.
4. After a few days, open the paper towel and look to see if the bean has sprouted.
5. Cut off the top third of the plastic bottle.
6. Poke a few holes in the bottom of the bottle using a pair of scissors or a knife. Place the bottle on top of a clean plate to catch the extra water that drains out.
7. Fill the bottle with potting soil and plant the newly sprouted bean a few inches down into the soil and up against the side of the bottle so you can see it growing.
8. Water the soil and place the bottle in a sunny window.
9. Keep the soil moist.

As the bean grows roots you can see them spread into the ground through the clear plastic. During the growing season, the bean plant can be planted outside, but it will need some kind of trellis, such as dead branches, that it can climb on.

Science Night

Turn your home into your own scientific laboratory. You'll be amazed at how many experiments you can conduct right in your own home. Everyone is curious about how things work and what makes things happen. Children and adults will learn a lot about science and the world around them on *Science Night!*

Newton's Racing Balloons

Legend has it that when an apple fell on Sir Isaac Newton's head, he was inspired to learn about gravity; that is, the way things fall and move. Here's a moving experiment you can conduct.

What You Need

* 2 pieces of string, long enough to span the distance from one wall to the opposite wall in the room where you are doing your experiment
* 2 soda straws
* Scissors
* Tape
* 2 latex balloons, large
* Clothespins or document clips
* A grown-up to assist

1. Thread a string through a straw, then tape each end of the string to opposite walls.
2. Thread another string through a second straw and tape it on the wall a few feet away from and parallel to the first string. (Note: If others are watching the experiment, place and tape one string lower than the other so that both can be seen.)
3. Blow up two balloons and clip them closed with clothespins or document clips.
4. Tape the side of each balloon to one of the two straws, with the clipped openings on the same side of the straw.

5. Push the balloons and straws all the way to one end of the string, with the balloon opening that is clipped facing the near wall. Now you are ready to race!
6. Release the clips at the same time. The balloons will expel the air in one direction, creating a force. The balloons taped to the straws will slide in the opposite direction with an equal force. How far each balloon travels depends on how straight the string is and how much the balloon is inflated.

For another experiment, try inflating each balloon differently, one with a lot of air and the other with half as much. Which one do you predict will go farther?

Sir Isaac Newton figured out that the way an object moves could be predicted according to three simple rules. One of these rules states that any action will produce an equal and opposite reaction. When some force is put on an object, that object pushes back in an equal amount, but in an opposite direction. Here you can see that when the air in the balloon blows out one way, the balloon is propelled in the opposite direction. By changing the amount of air pushing out in one direction, there is a stronger force pushing the balloon in the opposite direction.

Buckle Up Dolly

Newton's first rule of motion states that an object that is not moving will stay that way, and that an object in motion will stay in motion until acted upon by an outside force. That means if an object is moving one way it will keep moving in the same way until the object is sped up, slowed, or stopped, or until its direction is changed. This experiment will demonstrate Newton's rule.

What You Need

* Toy car with an open top and a removable doll passenger that can slide easily in and out of the seat

* Plank or a long, flat surface that can be raised into a ramp (must be wide enough for the toy car)

* Solid, heavy object about as big as the car

1. Place the car on a flat surface and watch what happens. Does it move if you don't push it? Newton said that an unmoving object will stay that way until a force makes it move.

2. Raise the plank high enough so that the car will move on its own when it is placed at the top of this newly constructed ramp. Place the car at the top of the ramp. Predict, just like a scientist, how far the car will travel when it is released. Let the car go. Notice how the car moves down the ramp and keeps going until it is stopped by something else or is slowed and stopped by the force of friction between the ground and the wheels. The higher the ramp, the greater the speed of the car, and the farther it will go.

3. Now place a heavy object at the bottom of the ramp and release the car at the top again. This time you'll see that an object that is too heavy for the toy car to push will suddenly stop the momentum of the car.

What would keep the doll safe inside the car when the car suddenly stops? A seatbelt!

4. Now place a doll into the seat of the car and again release it at the top of the ramp with the heavy object still at the bottom.

5. Discuss with other family members how many separate objects are moving. It is easy to think of the doll and the car as one object when they are pushed because they seem to move and stop at the same time. But it is important to know that the car and the doll are two separate objects that will each obey the laws of motion. So in this case, even if one object (the car) stops, the other (doll) keeps going. What will happen to the doll when the car is stopped by the heavy object? Release the car and find out. What often happens is the doll is thrown out of the car when the car suddenly stops. When the car and doll move down the ramp, they are moving at the same rate. When the motion of one of them (the car) suddenly changes, the other object (the doll) continues moving at the same rate in the same direction.

Kitchen Chemistry

Turn your kitchen into your scientific laboratory with this cool experiment.

What You Need

* Vinegar
* Measuring cup
* 1 or more plastic 2-liter bottles
* Funnel or paper cone
* Equal number of large latex balloons (large enough to stretch over the mouth of the bottle)
* Measuring spoons
* Baking soda
* A grown-up to assist
* Food coloring, optional
* Dishwashing soap, optional

1. Measure 1/2 cup vinegar and pour it into the plastic bottle.
2. Place a funnel or paper cone into one of the balloons.
3. Spoon about a tablespoon of baking soda into the balloon.
4. Remove the cone or funnel and stretch the balloon opening over the mouth of the plastic bottle.

If you are making more than one of these, count to three and lift the balloons up so the baking soda spills into the bottles at the same time.

Notice what happens when the baking soda and vinegar mix. There is a chemical reaction that changes each of these substances. One of the by-products of this reaction is carbon dioxide gas, which quickly fills the bottle and inflates the balloon. Baking soda and vinegar are chemicals. Baking soda is a powder known as sodium bicarbonate. The vinegar is a liquid known as acetic acid. When they mix together, they make three different substances. Two of the new substances are liquids: sodium acetate and water. The other substance is carbon dioxide gas. As the reaction creates carbon dioxide gas, it pushes the air already inside the bottle out and into the balloon.

You also can add some food coloring and a few squirts of dishwashing soap to the vinegar before you put in the baking soda. When the vinegar is poured in, the carbon dioxide gas will make colored soap bubbles. If there is enough gas, the bubbles will spew out of the top of the bottle.

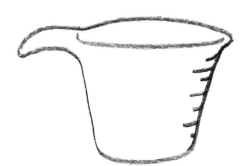

Fingerprints

You can do this activity on Mystery Night or Science Night. Watch out criminals, we're using science!

What You Need

* ❄ 1 or more aluminum soda cans, empty
* ❄ 1 or more resealable plastic bags, large enough to hold one soda can
* ❄ Super-strength bonding glue (such as Super Glue)
* ❄ A grown-up to assist

1. Wrap your hand around an empty soda can and be sure to get your fingerprints all over it.
2. Have an adult drop several drops of super-strength bonding glue into a corner of a resealable plastic bag.
3. Put the can in the bag, but not touching the glue.
4. Seal the bag and wait 20 minutes.
5. The fumes from the glue will stick to the oils left on the can by your fingers.
6. The pattern that shows up on the can will be your unique fingerprints.

You can also repeat this experiment by having two people touch the can and then repeat the steps above. Then see if you can match the fingerprints to each person.

Note: Don't open the bag after this experiment. Please put it in the trash when finished.

Air Everywhere

Here is a hot-air experiment to demonstrate how warmer gases are less dense than colder ones. When something is denser, that means it has more little pieces of it closer together (for example, a baseball), and often is heavier than a less dense thing (for example, a tennis ball). When some air is denser, it sinks down, and when some air is less dense, it rises up. This concept is used in hot-air balloons.

What You Need

* ❋ Hot-air popcorn popper or hair dryer
* ❋ Clean plastic bag, about the size of a tall kitchen garbage bag
* ❋ A grown-up to assist

1. Have a grown-up plug in and turn on a hot-air popcorn popper or a hair dryer set on low.

2. Place a plastic garbage bag over the popper or the dryer. Do not hold the bag closed; just hold it down so it doesn't blow away. Wait and watch. The popper and dryer both heat up the air inside the bag. As the air inside the bag gets warmer, the bag inflates and then floats up. As you feel the bag inflate with warmer air, let it go and see if it floats upward. Be careful as these appliances may become hot.

3. Turn off the popper or the dryer as soon as the bag begins to rise.

When something gets hotter, the tiny molecules of the substance begin to move more quickly. Molecules in a gas (such as the air) are already more spread out and moving faster than molecules in a liquid (such as water) or in a solid (such as a brick). At a normal temperature, some things are gases, with molecules spread out and moving fast. Other things at a normal temperature are liquids, with molecules closer together and moving slower. Still other things are solid at a normal temperature, with molecules really close together and not moving much at all.

When the molecules heat up, they spread out more, inflating the bag. Warmer gases are less dense than colder ones, so they will rise above colder gases, which are heavier. Warm air rises and carries the bag with it.

Lift

Lift is the principle of aerodynamics that helps an airplane or a bird to fly.

What You Need

* Rectangular shaped paper
* Toilet tissue roll, half-full
* Plunger
* High-speed hair dryer or small fan
* A grown-up to assist

1. Hold the paper up to your mouth with both hands, with the short side of the paper by your mouth. The rest of the paper will drop down.

2. Hold the edge of the paper between your lips and blow out hard. Watch the paper's position and see how it changes when you blow out air. What you are likely to see is the other end of the paper will rise up as you blow.

This is an example of lift. When air passes over a thin, solid surface, the airstream is cut in two; half of it goes over the surface, and the other half passes under it.

On an airplane wing, the top of the wing is curved while the bottom is flat. The difference in distance between the top of the wing and the bottom allows air moving over the wing to travel slower than the air moving under the wing. The air passing under the wing has faster moving pieces than the air above and so it moves upward, carrying the wing (and the airplane) with it.

Here's a more dramatic demonstration of lift.

1. Put the half-full roll of toilet paper on the handle of a plunger. Unroll the paper a little so it hangs down.

2. Two people hold the plunger, one on each end.

3. A third person holds a high-speed hair dryer or fan aimed at the toilet paper roll and pointed slightly upward to pass above it.

When turned on, the air will split over and under the toilet paper roll, with the air going under faster and creating lift. If the force of lift is strong enough, the end of the toilet paper will be unrolled into the sky.

Spa Night

This is a wonderfully relaxing family night, and it's not just for girls. Boys enjoy relaxing too, and there's nothing like a family massage circle!

Create a bin to keep all your *Spa Night* supplies together. When the family sees the bin, they'll know it's time for a night of fun relaxation. Your *Spa Night* bin might include washcloths for each family member, hair bands to tie your hair back, lotions, scented candles, a face mask, massage tools, and nail supplies.

Family members can do the activities in this chapter together at the same time, or rotate around different spa service "stations."

Set the mood for *Spa Night* with relaxing music. Music with calming sounds sets just the right mood. Classical music can be a good choice. Brew some herbal tea, light some candles (with a grown-up's help), put on your robes and slippers, and enjoy *Spa Night*.

Smoothies

A smoothie is a great spa snack. It can be made with yogurt for a healthy treat or with ice cream for a fun dessert.

What You Need

* ❋ 1 or more of the following: yogurt, milk, frozen yogurt, or ice cream
* ❋ 1 or more of your favorite fruits
* ❋ Blender
* ❋ Glass
* ❋ A grown-up to assist

Put the ingredients into a blender and blend until smooth. Poor into a glass and enjoy.

For an extra treat, make a sugar rim on your glass.

Sugar Rim

What You Need

* ❋ Sugar
* ❋ Small packet of powdered drink mix
* ❋ Bowl, small
* ❋ Spoon
* ❋ A slice of lemon or lime

1. Combine a few spoonfuls of sugar with a small packet of your favorite flavor of powdered drink mix in the bowl. Choose a flavor that will complement the flavor of your smoothie.

2. Before pouring the smoothie into your glass, run the lemon slice along the rim of the glass. This will make it moist and help the mixture stick to the rim of your glass.

3. Turn your glass upside down on top of the sugar mixture so that the rim is in the mixture. Twist the glass a bit to collect more of the mixture.

4. Turn the glass right side up, pour the smoothie inside the glass, and enjoy.

Foot Spa

You can get special foot spa products from the store or just use supplies you have around the house. Each family member can do this activity for himself or herself, or you can do it for each other. Any way you choose to do this activity, your feet will feel great after a family foot spa!

What You Need

❋ Small tubs or large buckets or pots filled with warm water

❋ Towels

❋ Bath salts (optional)

❋ Candy canes or other peppermint candies (optional)

❋ Soaps or foot washes

❋ Foot files (optional)

❋ Lotions (optional)

❋ Foot massagers, or a small ball (optional)

❋ Nail polish (optional)

❋ Slippers or cozy socks (optional)

❋ Nail clippers (optional)

❋ Nail file (optional)

❋ Cotton balls (optional)

❋ Flip-flops (optional)

❋ A grown-up to assist

1. Soak your feet in the warm water. If you like, you can add bath salts. Peppermint is a natural foot-relaxing ingredient, so you can crush up a candy cane and add it to your water if you like.

2. Wash your feet. Use foot wash or soap, and massage your feet as you wash them.

3. If you have a foot file, use it to rub your feet and get the skin extra clean and smooth.

4. Put lotion on your feet. Rub and massage the lotion into your feet, ankles, and calves—all the way up to your knees.

5. Use a foot massager or a small ball to massage the bottom of your feet by gently stepping on it and rolling your foot around on top of the ball while applying gentle pressure.

6. If you are not painting your toenails with polish, then go ahead and put on your slippers or a pair of cozy socks. If you are putting on nail polish, continue with step 7—the pedicure process.

7. Using nail clippers and a nail file, shape your toenails the way you want them.

8. Pull cotton balls apart to make a longer strand of cotton. Push it between your toes to separate them.

9. Apply a colored nail polish to your toenails.

10. Wait at least 20 minutes before doing anything else with your feet, such as putting on a pair of shoes. Then carefully remove the cotton and put on your flip-flops for the rest of Spa Night.

Enjoy your silky and beautiful feet!

Face Masks

You look pretty silly—even scary—in a face mask, but it is really good for your skin.

What You Need

* Bowls
* Spoons
* Cucumber slices (relieves puffiness and relaxes your eyes)
* Washcloths
* Any mixture of the following:

For dry skin

* Heavy cream
* Avocado
* Olive oil
* Sour cream

For normal skin

* Peach or plum
* Cornmeal, mixed with fruit (to help exfoliate the skin)
* Cooked oatmeal
* Mud

For oily skin

* Lemon or lime juice
* Egg whites mixed with honey
* Yogurt, plain
* Apple (pureed or can be cut open and rubbed directly on the skin)

For all types of skin

* Banana for cleansing and moisturizing (Banana is recommended for all skin types, and is believed to have some healing powers. Some people use banana on burns)

For the hair

* Plastic wrap
* Egg

It took 90 makeup artists to help Jim Carrey into his makeup for *The Grinch*. The process took up to two hours every day.

These ingredients have nutrients that are good for your face and skin. You can experiment with different combinations of them to see which ones you like best. You don't need to use a lot. Just a couple of teaspoons of each ingredient will go a long way.

Mix up the ingredients you have chosen into a small bowl. Using your fingers, apply the mixture to your face. Be careful not to get it too close to your eyes. After the mask is on, lie back, close your eyes, and place the cucumber slices over your eyes. Relax for at least 10 minutes. Then, take off the cucumber slices and use a wet washcloth to wipe off the mask.

Egg is also a good conditioner for your hair. Scramble one egg with a fork and then mix it into your hair (over a kitchen sink), then cover your hair with plastic wrap for 10 minutes before rinsing it out. Now shower and shampoo your hair for a silky texture.

Manicures

Manicures are not just for pretty nails. They make your entire hand feel good, and you don't have to put on polish if you don't want to. You can do your manicure while your feet are soaking and before your pedicure.

If you want to get serious, you can purchase manicure tools from a drug store, such as cuticle cutters and cuticle pushers, but don't worry if you don't have these things. You can still make your hands look and feel great. This is a good activity for each child to play safely with a parent.

What You Need

* Nail clippers
* Nail file
* Lotion
* Cuticle cream or oil (optional)
* Cuticle cutter (optional)
* Cuticle pusher (optional)
* Nail brush
* Nail polish, clear (optional)
* Nail polish, including base coat and top coat (optional)

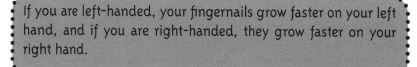

1. Shape your nails. Use the nail clippers to make them the length you want. Clip them so that they are all around the same length. Then use the nail file to shape them.

2. Apply lotion to your hands. Massage the lotion into your hands. If you are wearing any rings, you might want to take them off. Go all the way up your arms, massaging as you go. Pull on each finger as you massage the fingers. This is good for circulation.

3. Put cuticle cream or oil on your cuticles (at the base of your nail), and rub it in. This strengthens your nails and helps them grow. At this time, you can cut or push back your cuticles, which will also help keep your nails strong.

If you are left-handed, your fingernails grow faster on your left hand, and if you are right-handed, they grow faster on your right hand.

4. Wash your hands. If you have a nail brush, use it to get your nails extra clean.

5. Dry your nails well before starting to apply polish. If you don't want colorful nails, but you want them to look nice, apply some clear nail polish. If you do want colorful nails, continue.

6. Apply a base coat. This helps the color stay on your nails.

7. Apply two coats of the color. Don't apply it too thick. Just a little bit goes a long way. Don't worry if you paint off the nail. You can use a nail stick to get the polish off your finger. Even if you accidentally leave some polish on your fingers, it will probably come off in the bath or shower, so don't worry.

8. Apply a top coat.

Don't touch anything for 20 minutes after your manicure. You may also blow on your nails to help them dry.

Massages

There are a lot of ways to enjoy a massage, and different people like different things. Some people like firm massages; others like them gentle. Some like their shoulders rubbed; others their feet. Here are some ways to discover your favorite type of massage.

Massage Circle

Sit on the floor in a tight circle with your family, with your back to the person on your right. Make sure the circle is tight enough that you can comfortably reach the person in front of you. Massage that person's shoulders, while the person behind you massages your shoulders, and so on, so that everyone is getting and giving a massage at the same time. Try different techniques as you rub their shoulders, such as kneading (squeezing), gentle hits with the side of your hand, or magic fingers. To do magic fingers use the tips of your fingers and walk with them all along the other person's back. After a while, turn around so that you are massaging the person who was massaging you, and vice versa.

Focusing on One-Person Massage

One family member lies down and the others gather around him or her. Each family member massages a different area of his body at the same time.

Depending on how many people you have, you might divide up as follows: someone take his left arm, someone else his left leg and foot, another his right side, and one person his head. (When massaging someone's head you can start with the scalp. Gently massage under the hair and all around the head.) Also, you can place two of your fingers on the person's temples (to the sides of the eyes) and gently rub in circles.

Take turns being the person getting the massage.

> The skin is the largest organ of the human body.

Pressure Points

Reflexology is based on the belief that the parts of your body have certain connections to other parts. Try massaging different areas of your feet in order to help other areas of your body. Let each family member name a part of his or her body he or she would like to feel better, and see if you can make the person feel better by massaging a part of that person's foot instead. Here is a table to show you how reflexology is believed to work:

Massaging this . . .	Makes this feel better . . .
The tips of the toes	*head and sinuses*
The big toe	*neck*
Just below the toes	*ears*
The bridge of the foot	*lungs and chest*
The upper and outer ridge	*arms and shoulders*
The ball of the foot	*stomach*
The heel	*back*

Acupressure

Acupressure is similar to reflexology, only the belief is that the pressure points can help your mind and mental well-being in addition to your body. Massage or put pressure on the body part and see if it helps improve other feelings. Here is a table to show you how acupressure may work:

Fourth toe .... *decision making, forgiveness*
Inside of foot .... *willpower and courage*
Elbow .... *anger management*
Big toe .... *self-esteem*
Below the big toe .... *relaxation, happiness*
Palm, wrist, and upper arm .... *relief from grief*
Ear.. *focus*
Top of hand, palm side of wrist..................................... *calm*
Under pinky finger.. *concentration*

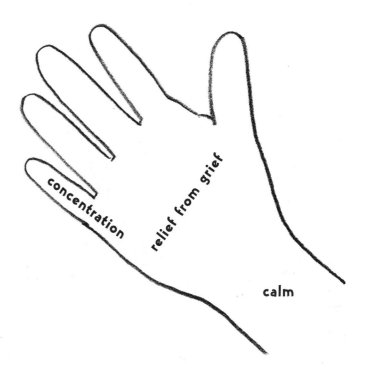

Formal Night

Why wait for a special occasion? Get out your fancy clothes and have a Formal Night tonight! Getting dressed up always makes you feel special, and sometimes it's important to feel that way, even if you're not going anywhere.

You may see Mom and Dad getting all dressed up for a wedding or a fancy party, but why should Mom and Dad have all the fun? Use the good china, practice fancy table manners, light some candles (with a grown-up's help), and enjoy Formal Night.

Decorate Candles

Nothing says fancy like beautiful candles. Your family can beautify your own candles for Formal Night. There are many different ways to beautify candles. Here are a few. They all start with basic white candles.

Crayon Candles

What You Need

* Newspaper
* Crayons
* Pots
* White candlesticks
* Paintbrushes
* A grown-up to assist

1. Place sheets of newspaper on a tabletop to protect it.
2. Take the labels off the crayons.
3. Place similar color crayons in a pot; separate different colors into different pots.
4. Melt the crayons on the stove over a low heat.
5. Once the crayons are melted, turn off the heat. Put the white candles on the table and use paintbrushes to brush the melted crayon wax onto the candles. Be careful—the melted wax is hot!

Wikki Stick Candles

What You Need

* Wikki sticks (thin strips of molding wax, often found in toy stores)

1. Take a Wikki stick and wrap it around a candle in a design.
2. Press it into the wax to affix.

Stamp Candles

What You Need

* Newspaper
* Ink stamps
* Ink pad
* Tissue paper
* Hair dryer
* White candlesticks
* A grown-up to assist

1. Place sheets of newspaper on a tabletop to protect it.
2. Select an ink stamp and press it into the ink pad.
3. Press the inked stamp onto a piece of tissue paper in various places.
4. Once dry, wrap the tissue paper around a candlestick, wrapping it around only one time.
5. Hold the candle at the tip. Put the the hair dryer on the highest setting and blow the hot air onto the tissue-paper-wrapped candle. The tissue paper will melt into the candle.
6. Cut off any tissue paper that is not attached to the candle so there is no paper hanging off.

Here's a candle tip: Place your candles in the freezer for an hour before burning them. They'll last much longer.

Dress Up

Put on your fanciest clothes. Mom, here's a chance to wear an old bridesmaid's dress again. Dad, don't forget your tie! Hats and gloves will make your Formal Night even fancier.

Keep a bin of dress-up clothes handy, ready for formal time at any time. Here are ideas for things you can keep in your dress-up bin:

❋ Fancy gloves

❋ Fancy hats

❋ Silky scarves to wear in your hair, over the shoulder, around your neck, or around your waist

❋ Capes, a great fancy accessory

❋ Old tutus or other dance costumes

❋ Feather boas

❋ Fake pearl necklaces

❋ Crowns and tiaras

❋ Fancy shoes

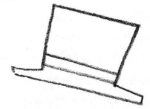

Actress Glenn Close, who played Cruella DeVil in *101 Dalmatians*, insisted on keeping her costume from the movie. She collects movie costumes.

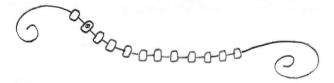

Place Cards

You might want to prepare an especially fancy table for dinner on Formal Night, and place cards will add a touch of elegance. Place cards show where everyone will sit. Use different names so each person has to figure out where he or she sits. Then it's not only formal, but fun! Here are some ideas:

Letter jumble. Jumble the letters in each person's name. For example, Brian becomes Nirab, and Wanda become Adwan.

First letter. Put on the place card the name of a famous celebrity or fictional character whose name starts with the same first letter as your family member's name. For example, Martin becomes Mickey Mouse, and Sarah becomes Snow White.

What happened on your birthday. Write on the place card a historical event that happened on each family member's birthday. For example, if your birthday is April 15, write "The Titanic Sunk." You can go online to find out other historical dates.

Same birthday. You can also look on the Internet to find celebrities or famous people who share the birthday of a family member.

Top song, movie, or actor. Write on the place card a song, movie, or actor that was popular the year each family member was born. Go to www.multied.com/20th for top songs and movies by year in the 20th century, as well as lists of Nobel prize winners, sports figures, popular books, and television programs. Go to www.film-center.com/a1_hist.html for a listing of Academy Award winners by year.

Family members may not figure out which place card is which at first, but the place cards will make good conversation starters.

Before dinner plates were invented, people used to eat their food off thick pieces of bread.

Waltzing

Fancy dancing is an important part of any formal affair.

You'll need some music in 3/4 time; that is, music that has three beats per measure (counting one, two, three before the pattern repeats). There are many classical music pieces you can play; many of them have the word *waltz* in the title. If you don't have classical music, there are other kinds of songs in 3/4 time. The Beatles' "She's Leaving Home" is a good example because it's not too fast and not too slow for beginning waltz dancers.

You can turn the music on and just have some fun dancing with your partner, or you can actually learn to waltz. Here's how:

The leader puts his right hand on his partner's left shoulder blade, and holds her right hand with his left hand. The "follower" puts her left hand on her partner's right shoulder.

The leader steps forward with his left foot (one), then forward with his right foot (two), and then brings his left foot to his right foot (three). Then he does the same thing on the other side: forward with his right foot (one), forward with his left foot (two), right foot to left foot (three).

The follower steps back with her right foot (one), then back with her left foot (two), then brings her right foot to her left foot (three). Then does the same thing on the other side: Back with her left foot (one), back with her right foot (two), left foot to right foot (three); that is the mirror of the leader's moves.

After you get used to those steps, try turning around in a circle while keeping the same footing.

Composer Johann Strauss wrote more than 400 waltzes.

Names, Accents, and Entrances

In India, women in royal families change their clothes several times a day, and give their worn-only-once clothes to their workers.

After you are dressed, create a fancy name for yourself. For example, if your names are Sherry and Lisa, you could say they are Shalandra and Liza. You can also use your middle name as your first name and the street you live on as your last name. For example, if your middle name is Leigh and you live on Asbury Avenue, your fancy name could be Leigh Asbury.

Try speaking with a fancy accent. A royal British accent can be very fancy. Think of Mary Poppins or Harry Potter and try to speak as they do. You can say "spit, spot!" and "Oh, really!" just like the British do. Another good accent for Formal Night is a southern accent. Think of the movies *Gone with the Wind* or *Oklahoma!* and try to talk like those characters do.

Have one member of the family announce your name and where you are from as you make a grand entrance in your beautiful dress-up clothes: "Ladies and Gentleman, the Royal Princess Michaela of Glenview."

Be sure to use your best manners all night as you say "How do you do?" and "I am pleased to have made your acquaintance" when you are first introduced to a fellow dinner guest (even if you already know him or her).

Make Punch

Break out the fancy glasses and a big punch bowl. If you don't have a punch bowl, any large bowl will do. Here are some punch recipes:

Royal Red Punch

What You Need

* ❋ 1 2-liter bottle of cherry-flavored carbonated soda
* ❋ 1 large bottle of cranberry/raspberry juice
* ❋ 1 cup of strawberries, raspberries, or any of your favorite berries
* ❋ Ice
* ❋ Punch bowl
* ❋ Large spoon for mixing
* ❋ Ladle
* ❋ Cups

1. Measure out all the ingredients.
2. Mix all the ingredients into the punch bowl.
3. Serve in cups over ice.

Mimosa Punch

What You Need

* ❋ 1 2-liter bottle of clear carbonated beverage
* ❋ 1/2 gallon of orange juice
* ❋ Ice
* ❋ Punch bowl
* ❋ Spoon
* ❋ 1 orange
* ❋ Cutting board
* ❋ Knife
* ❋ Ladle
* ❋ Cups
* ❋ A grown-up to assist

1. Place the clear carbonated beverage, orange juice, and ice in the punch bowl. Stir to mix.
2. Slice the orange into thin round slices in the shape of the sun.
3. Place the orange slices on top of the punch mixture and serve, or fill cups with the punch mixture and place one orange slice on the top of each cup.

Rainbow Punch

What You Need

* Punch bowl
* 1/2 gallon of fruit punch
* Ice
* 1 pint rainbow sherbet
* 1 2-liter bottle of clear carbonated beverage
* Ladle
* Cups

1. Place the fruit punch, ice, and sherbet in the punch bowl.
2. Pour the carbonated beverage over the sherbet. Watch the sherbet foam.
3. Ladle the punch into cups and serve.

Bert Lahr, in his cowardly lion costume for *The Wizard of Oz*, couldn't open his mouth wide enough to eat. His food was pureed in a blender, and he'd take sips of it through a straw during breaks.

Banana Split Punch

What You Need

* Punch bowl
* 1/2 gallon milk
* 8-ounce jar of chocolate syrup
* Bowl
* 2 bananas
* Knife
* 6 to 12 cherries
* 1 can whipped cream
* Spoon
* Ladle
* Cups
* A grown-up to assist

1. Pour the milk and chocolate syrup into the bowl.
2. Slice the bananas and add to the bowl.
3. Add the cherries to the bowl.
4. Top with whipped cream.
5. Ladle into cups and serve.

Ice Sculptures

No formal night would be complete without an ice sculpture as a table centerpiece.

What You Need

* Jell-O molds in fun shapes
* Shallow pan, plate, or cookie sheet
* Ice cubes
* Spoons
* Water

1. Fill the Jell-O molds with water and freeze to get fun-shaped ice cubes.
2. Using the pan, plate, or cookie sheet as your base, build a sculpture with these fun-shaped ice cubes and regular ice cubes. You can use a spoon to chip away at the ice to create different shapes.
3. Sprinkle water on the ice cubes to get them to stick to each other, or a bit more water to melt the ice cubes a little. The sculptures will be abstract and unique.
4. Display your sculpture throughout Formal Night. Watch how it changes shape as it melts.

> The Roman Emperor Nero used to send for fresh snow from the mountains to be made into royal ice cream.

Masquerades

Some formal parties are masquerade balls. The guests wear masks, but not like Halloween masks. These masks are beautiful and fancy. You can make your own masquerade party mask. Place it on your dinner table and hold it over your face whenever you talk. This can be challenging and fun.

What You Need

* Paper plates
* Scissors
* Glue
* Sticks
* Feathers and/or other craft supplies like pom-poms, glitter, and sequins
* Pencil
* Markers or paint
* Tape
* A grown-up to assist

1. Cut a paper plate in half. One half will be the base for your mask.
2. Hold one half up to your face with the curved side at the top of your face.
3. Measure spaces for your eyes. Mark with a pencil.
4. Cut out two holes for your eyes.
5. Color or paint your mask and glue decorations onto it.
6. Tape the stick to the unpainted side of the mask on the side. Let it dry.
7. Use the stick to hold the mask up to your face.

Jewelry Night

One of my favorite things to do with my grandma was to look through all of her old jewelry. She'd let me try everything on, and tell me the origin of each piece of jewelry—some were gifts from family members, and some were birthday, Valentine's Day, or other holiday gifts. Others were gifts from her third-grade students. Some were from my grandfather.

Because of my memories of sharing these times with my grandmother, Jewelry Night is special in my house.

You can make jewelry, or you can tell stories about the jewelry you have. You might learn a lot about your family, or create a special heirloom of your own!

Making Jewelry

There are many different ways to make jewelry, and dozens of kits you can purchase with tools to create jewelry of all kinds. Here are two types of jewelry that are easy to make.

Beaded Jewelry

What You Need

* String, thread, thin wire, or yarn (depending on the size of your beads)
* Scissors
* Beads
* Needle for threading small beads, if desired
* Fasteners, if desired
* A grown-up to assist

1. Measure your wrist or neck with a piece of string, thread, thin wire, or yarn. Cut it to the length you want the jewelry to be plus a few extra inches (for good measure).
2. Tie a knot at one end of the string.
3. Thread the beads onto your string. If they are small beads, you may need to use a needle to get them onto your wire or thread. Tie a knot at the other end, and then tie the two knotted ends together. For tighter jewelry, use fasteners instead of knots.

> During the Renaissance, rings set with precious stones were thought to have magical powers.

Pipe Cleaner Flower Rings

These are fun and furry pieces of ring jewelry.

What You Need

* Colored pipe cleaners

1. Choose two different colors of pipe cleaners.
2. Hold them together and twist them in the center so that they spiral around each other for a couple of inches. (They will look like a candy cane.)
3. Place the top of your finger, where you wear a ring, in the middle of the pipe cleaners (the twisted part) and wrap the pipe cleaners once around your finger. Twist the pipe cleaner once to secure your finger size.
4. Take the pipe cleaner off your finger and untwist any part past the ring part. Make sure the colors alternate.
5. Roll up each of the four ends into the middle to create flower petals.

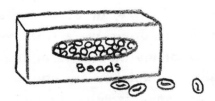

Beads

Stones and Stories

In Jerusalem, 12 gems decorating a castle wall were divided into the 12 months. These are the original birthstones. Birthstones have changed from country to country and over time. In the 18th century there were different birthstone categories, which included Arabian, Hindu, Jewish, Polish, and Russian. In the 20th century, traditional American and European birthstones were added. Here is a list of the modern American birthstones, and their meanings.

January: Garnet (deep burgundy), meaning faith, eternity, and truth

February: Amethyst (purple), meaning luck, wit, and health

March: Aquamarine (pale blue), meaning happiness, understanding, and everlasting youth

April: Diamond (clear), meaning eternity, courage, and health

May: Emerald (deep green), meaning fidelity, goodness, and love

June: Pearl or Moonstone (light pink), meaning peace, nobility, and beauty

July: Ruby (red), meaning love, enthusiasm, and strength

August: Peridot (yellow), meaning success, peace, and luck

September: Sapphire (deep blue) meaning serenity, truth, and noble soul

October: Opal or Tourmaline (pink), meaning purity, hope, and health

November: Topaz (orange), meaning wisdom, courage, and sincerity

December: Turquoise (blue), meaning love, happiness, and luck

Most people know their birthstone, but did you know that the days of the week have stones, too? In Thailand, for example, fashion dictates that certain colors of clothing and jewelry be worn on different days of the week:

Sunday: Sunstone (yellow)

Monday: Moonstone (pink)

Tuesday: Sapphire (deep blue)

Wednesday: Ruby (red)

Thursday: Cat's-Eye (black)

Friday: Alexandrite (pink)

Saturday: Labradorite (gray)

To tell jewelry stories, choose a piece of jewelry, and tell your family a story about its meaning or about where you acquired it.

> The emerald (May's birthstone) is known to be the favorite of royalty. It's considered a symbol of success.

Candy Necklaces

Try to finish making this necklace before you eat it!

What You Need

* String (elastic string works best)
* Scissors
* Piece of cardboard
* Hard round candies, pieces of round cereal, or other sweets that have holes in the middle
* A grown-up to assist

1. Measure the string to fit around your neck. Make sure it's long enough to slip over your head.
2. Cut the string about 1/2 inch longer than your desired final length. Tie a double (or larger) knot at one end.
3. Cut out a small circle of cardboard, larger than the food you will be stringing. Use the point of one of the scissor blades to make a small hole in the center and add it to the end of the string, just on top of the knot. (This will keep your sweet treats from falling off the necklace and keep the knots secured.)
4. String the food pieces onto your string. Knot the other end, and then tie the knots together. Slip the string over your head, and enjoy your necklace.

In Vietnam everyone's birthday is celebrated on New Year's Day. They call it Tet. A baby turns one on Tet no matter when he or she was born that year. On the first morning of Tet (the holiday lasts for three days), adults present their children with red envelopes that contain what they call lucky money.

Fancy Princess (or Prince) Game

The object of this game is to collect your necklace, bracelet, ring, and the crown to win. But you cannot win if you have the Evil Ring!

What You Need

* 1 crown
* Necklace, 1 for each player
* 1 ring to be designated as the Evil Ring
* 1 die
* Bracelet, 1 for each player
* Ring, 1 for each player

Pick one ring to be the Evil Ring. Place all of the jewelry and the crown into the middle of the table. All players sit around the pile of jewelry. Take turns rolling the die and collecting the jewelry according to the number rolled and the meaning of each number as shown here:

1: Retrieve your necklace
2: Retrieve your bracelet
3: Retrieve your ring
4: Retrieve the Evil Ring (you cannot win with this piece)
5: Retrieve the crown
6: Retrieve any piece

1. For the rolls of either 4 or 5—the Evil Ring and the crown—you take them, even if they are in another player's own pile of jewelry.
2. Wear each piece of jewelry as you earn it in the game.
3. The first player to have all of his or her jewelry, including the crown (but not the Evil Ring) wins!

Spooky Night

Sometimes it's fun to be scared together. Your family will want to stick very close to each other during Spooky Night. Turn the lights down low and get out your flashlight to enjoy your own haunted house. This fun-filled night is not just for Halloween.

Put on some spooky music such as "Monster Mash" or the soundtrack to *The Nightmare Before Christmas*. Make shadow puppets and noises, have a séance, become a mummy, eat scary sweet treats, and more. Don't be too afraid. There's safety in numbers, and you're with your family. So enjoy Spooky Night!

Here are some scary movies that the whole family can watch:
* *Haunted Mansion*
* *The Addams Family*
* *Addams Family Values*
* *The Nightmare Before Christmas*
* *Scooby Doo*

Shadow Puppet Storytelling

What You Need

* Flashlight
* A white wall or white sheet for projecting shadows
* A room that can get very dark
* Paper
* Scissors
* Glue or tape
* Tongue-depressor sticks or Popsicle sticks
* A grown-up to assist

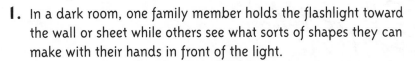

1. In a dark room, one family member holds the flashlight toward the wall or sheet while others see what sorts of shapes they can make with their hands in front of the light.

2. Try shaping your hand to make one of the following animals:

    * Bunny
    * Snake
    * Dog
    * Worms hatching
    * Monster
    * Alligator

3. You can also make shadow puppets out of paper. Cut out a shape and glue or tape it onto a stick. Use the shadow puppets to tell stories. See how the puppet projection on the wall gets bigger or smaller as you hold the flashlight nearer to and farther away from the puppet. Make up a scary story about a creature, such as a spider, that keeps getting bigger.

> The Broadway show of Disney's *The Lion King* uses more than 230 puppets. Some of them are shadow puppets.

Tell "The Old Woman Who Swallowed a Fly" story as a shadow puppet play. Here is a list of the characters you'll need to make for the story.

* Fly
* Spider
* Bird
* Cat
* Dog
* Goat
* Cow
* Horse
* Old woman with a big open mouth

Now you're ready for the script. Re-create each shadow puppet as each appears in the story as indicated below.

I knew an old woman who swallowed a fly (*make the shadow projection of the fly look like it's going into the old woman's mouth*).
I don't know why she swallowed the fly.
Perhaps she'll die.

I knew an old woman who swallowed a spider. (*Make the shadow projection of the spider look like it's going into the old woman's mouth.*)
That wiggled and jiggled and tickled inside her.
She swallowed the spider to catch the fly.
But I don't know why she swallowed the fly.
Perhaps she'll die.

I knew an old woman who swallowed a bird. (*Make the shadow projection of the bird look like it's going into the old woman's mouth.*)
How absurd, to swallow a bird!
She swallowed the bird to catch the spider
That wiggled and jiggled and tickled inside her.
She swallowed the spider to catch the fly.
But I don't know why she swallowed the fly.
Perhaps she'll die.

I knew an old lady who swallowed a cat. (*Make the shadow projection of the cat look like it's going into the old woman's mouth.*)
Imagine that! She swallowed a cat.
She swallowed the cat to catch the bird.
She swallowed the bird to catch the spider
That wiggled and jiggled and tickled inside her.
She swallowed the spider to catch the fly.
But I don't know why she swallowed the fly.
Perhaps she'll die.

I knew an old lady who swallowed a dog. (*Make the shadow projection of the dog look like it's going into the old woman's mouth.*)
What a hog to swallow a dog!
She swallowed the dog to catch the cat.
She swallowed the cat to catch the bird.
She swallowed the bird to catch the spider
That wiggled and jiggled and tickled inside her.
She swallowed the spider to catch the fly.
But I don't know why she swallowed the fly.
Perhaps she'll die.

I knew an old lady who swallowed a goat. (*Make the shadow projection of the goat look like it's going into the old woman's mouth.*)
She opened her throat, and swallowed a goat.
She swallowed the goat to catch the dog.
She swallowed the dog to catch the cat.
She swallowed the cat to catch the bird.
She swallowed the bird to catch the spider
That wiggled and jiggled and tickled inside her.
She swallowed the spider to catch the fly.
But I don't know why she swallowed the fly.
Perhaps she'll die.

I knew an old lady who swallowed a cow. (*Make the shadow projection of the cow look like it's going into the old woman's mouth.*)
I don't know how she swallowed a cow!
She swallowed the cow to catch the goat.
She swallowed the goat to catch the dog.
She swallowed the dog to catch the cat.
She swallowed the cat to catch the bird.
She swallowed the bird to catch the spider
That wiggled and jiggled and tickled inside her.
She swallowed the spider to catch the fly.
But I don't know why she swallowed the fly.
Perhaps she'll die.

I knew an old lady who swallowed a horse. (*Make the shadow projection of the horse look like it's going into the old woman's mouth.*)
She's dead, of course. (*Make the old lady puppet fall over dead.*)

What's That Noise?

What You Need

* Flashlight

Take turns making a spooky sound with your voice, and have others guess what the sound is. Here are some suggestions:

* Creaky door
* Ghost's moan
* Witch's cackle
* Heartbeat
* Thunder
* Rattling bones
* Footsteps
* Werewolf's growl
* Black cat's screech
* Snake's hiss
* Monster's roar
* Owl's hoot
* Dracula's laugh
* Mouse's squeak
* Chattering teeth

1. After everyone has made up some spooky sounds, start a story that uses all of the sounds. Hold the flashlight under your chin, lighting up the rest of your face.
2. Point the flashlight to show whose turn it is to continue the story.
3. When a spooky sound is mentioned in the story, everyone makes the sound with his or her voice. Pass the flashlight around and let each person start a new story.

The book *Frankenstein* was written by Mary Wollstonecraft Shelley when her family had a writing night. The parents asked everyone to write a story.

Séance

If you could talk to Abraham Lincoln, what would you say? A séance is a ceremony during which some people believe you can speak to the dead. Whether you believe it or not, it's fun to imagine what you might ask Cleopatra if you could.

What You Need

* Ouija board (optional)
* Candles
* A grown-up to assist

1. Have a grown-up light some candles.
2. Turn out the lights.
3. Have everyone in the family sit in a circle on the floor and hold hands. (If you are using a Ouija board, two family members will have to put their fingers on the indicator. The others should hold hands.)
4. Decide on a ghost you'd like to talk to.
5. Have everyone concentrate on that person.
6. Say that person's name over and over again.
7. Take turns asking that person a question. Leave time in between questions to imagine what the answer might be.

After everyone has asked a question, turn the lights back on, and talk about what you imagined the answers to be. Did you feel like there might really have been a ghost in the room? Did it feel colder than usual? Did you feel any breezes? Did the candle-light flicker in an unusual way? Did you hear any strange noises? These are all things that some people say happen when there is a ghost nearby.

Monster Cupcakes

Here's a deliciously scary treat. Create the creepiest monster cupcake you can imagine!

What You Need

* Cupcakes from a package mix, baked and cooled
* Frosting, chocolate and vanilla
* Food coloring, green or red (optional)
* Spoons
* Edible foods for decorating such as tubes of icing (various colors), gummy worms, candy-coated chocolate, candy corn, licorice, and raisins
* A grown-up to assist

1. If you like, mix a few drops of green or red food coloring into the white vanilla frosting to make gruesome green or blood-red frosting. Pile the frosting onto a cupcake with a spoon.
2. Top your monster with candy-coated chocolates or raisins for eyes, candy corn teeth, gummy worm hair, and anything else you can dream up.

In ancient Egypt, children played with dolls, tops, and stuffed leather balls. They had board games with moves determined by the throw of dice.

Mummy Wraps

What You Need

* Rolls of toilet tissue

1. Use rolls of toilet tissue to wrap each person in your family like a mummy. You can have contests to see who can get unwrapped the fastest, or who can try to dance to the song "Monster Mash" without the toilet tissue falling off. See if you can wrap a family member up without breaking the roll; make it one continuous strand.
2. Then, to unravel, have the "mummy" spin around and around while you wrap the tissue back up.

It could take ancient Egyptians six to eight months to finish wrapping a mummy.

Ghost Story Food

On Spooky Night, we like to eat with the ghosts in our family. If an ancestor or family member has passed away and you know what his or her favorite food was, plan to eat that food on Spooky Night. As you eat the food, tell stories about that person and share memories. Perhaps their ghost will join you in your feast.

My grandmother always had certain kinds of mints. The smell and taste of those mints remind me of her. I like to serve those mints on Spooky Night and imagine she is nearby. My grandfather always shared ice cream with me. Now we tell stories about him whenever we eat his favorite flavor.

Fortune-Telling Night

Can you predict the future? It's fun to try. What can you tell about someone by the palm of his or her hand? This evening everyone can be a gypsy and see into the future. Drink tea made from loose tea leaves—some people believe they can tell your fortune by reading tea leaves. If your family enjoys Fortune-Telling night, you may want to get a deck of Tarot cards and Rune stones to further explore fortune-telling fun. Whether you believe in psychic ability or enjoy wondering what the future might hold, a Fortune-Telling Night can be a lot of fun for the entire family.

Gypsy Dance

What You Need

* Scarves and bandanas
* Polka or square-dancing music
* Tambourines (You can make a tambourine by gluing small bells onto the edges of a paper plate.)
* Bells
* Jewelry with bells, such as anklets

1. Tie a bandana around your head and knot it at the back of your neck.
2. Tie a scarf around your waist.
3. Play the music.
4. Dance around in a circle with other family members, using the tambourines and bells.
5. Play call and response. One family member taps out a rhythm with his or her tambourine. You can tap on your head, your shoulder, your knee, or any part of your body, in any rhythm you like, for others to copy. The other family members echo your rhythm, and tap it out the same way you did. Take turns being the leader.

Can you imagine dancing for more than three days straight? The world record for the longest period of continuous dancing in a dance marathon is 73 hours.

Fortune-Telling Fish

Electric eels are one of the only kinds of fish that can swim backward and forward.

What You Need

* Cellophane
* Scissors
* A grown-up to assist

1. Cut the cellophane into the shape of a small fish, about three inches long and one inch wide.
2. Hold it in the palm of your hand—don't close your hand—and wait. The fish moves magically (or perhaps it moves from the heat or moisture in your hand or air movement in the room). The way the fish moves is said to indicate the way you feel. Here are the interpretations:

Head moves: jealous
Tail moves: relaxed
Head and tail move: loving
Sides curl: confused
Motionless: sad
Curls up: passionate

Fortune-Telling Cards

What You Need

✳ Deck of cards

1. Select the person who will get his or her fortune told.

2. The selected person should think about and select four people to be the focus of his or her questions. It's most fun when the people chosen are present, but they don't need to be there for this to be a fun activity.

3. Pull out a king or queen from each of the four suits to represent each person you choose. For example, your mother may be represented by the queen of hearts; Dad, the king of diamonds; sister, the queen of spades; and brother, the king of clubs.

4. Lay these four cards out and face up in front of the fortune-teller.

5. The person whose fortune is being told shuffles the remaining cards and hands them to the fortune-teller.

6. The person who is having his or her fortune told then asks a question. This question must be answerable by one of the four people represented by the face cards. See below for examples.

7. Starting on the left, the fortune-teller turns over one card from the deck just below the first represented card (the queen of hearts). If the card turned over is a heart, the fortune-teller stops there. That means that Mom is the answer to the question (because Mom is the queen of hearts). If it is not a heart, the fortune-teller continues laying out cards beneath the other representative cards, in order, until one of the suits match. If, for example, a diamond card is turned over below the king of diamonds, then Dad is the answer, and so on.

8. Continue asking questions until all of the cards are used up.

Here are some examples of questions you might want to ask:

Who will give me the best birthday present?
Who is the neatest person?
Who will make me laugh next?
Who will I most look like when I'm older?
Who is the best cook?
Who is the most talented?
Who is the most athletic?
Who is the silliest?
Who is most likely to write a book?
Who is most likely to be on television?
Who is most likely to have an operation?
Who will be the next person to get sick?
Who has a secret?
Who is best at keeping a secret?

After all of the cards have been played, take each family member's pile of cards (the cards below their representative card) and divide the pile according to suit. Each suit represents a characteristic about that person.

Hearts: love

Diamonds: money

Spades: fun

Clubs: fights

Here's how you interpret each characteristic:

0 to 2 cards of a suit = You have a very little bit of this characteristic.

3 to 4 cards of the suit = You have an average amount of this characteristic.

5 or more cards of the suit = You have an above average amount of the suit.

For example, if there were five hearts beneath and including the queen of hearts, and if this card is for your mother, then that means she possesses an above average amount of love; two diamonds means she has very little money; three spades means she is an average amount of fun, and so forth.

Predictions

What will the future be like? No one really knows, but it's fun to try and guess. Take turns talking about the predictions you and your other family members have about the future. Designate one person as the question asker and then take turns answering and asking the questions if you like. Tell your prediction about a:

* New invention
* Trend
* Historical event
* New law
* Movie title
* Name of a soon-to-be-famous band
* New dance
* Celebrity who will pass away

You can write down everyone's predictions and then everyone casts votes on which predictions they believe will come true and which won't. Seal the predictions in an envelope and write, "To be opened on _____ (date)" one year later. When that anniversary date arrives, open the envelope and see how many of these predictions came true.

Palm Readings

Look at each other's palms and see what you can tell by the lines in each person's hands.
See the chart below for the meaning of each line.

The heart line (line A in the illustration) is the top horizontal line.

This line indicates love. The higher the line is, the more passionate, and sometimes jealous, the person is. A heart line that runs horizontally across the hand suggests a person who doesn't like to let emotions show—a person who is very controlled. A line that curves upward toward the index finger indicates a warm-hearted, reasonable, and affectionate person.

The head line (line B) is the middle horizontal line.

This line indicates intelligence. Any space between where the head line and the life line (line C) begin indicates how cautious a person is. When the lines are joined at the beginning it indicates a person who has a cautious and sometimes fearful nature. The further apart these lines are, the more confident and risk taking the person is.

The life line (line C) is the curved line that goes from the base of the palm to the point between the thumb and the first finger.

A life line that is more toward the middle of the palm indicates a person with a giving nature in love. The closer the life line is to the thumb, the less generous a person is with his or her energy and time.

> The palms of your hands and the soles of your feet contain the most sweat glands of any part of the body.

The passive hand (the hand that you don't use to write with) is read for inherited characteristics and potential. Differences between the two palms indicate a person who has actively worked toward self-development.

For more detailed palm reading ideas visit www.ofesite.com/spirit/palm.

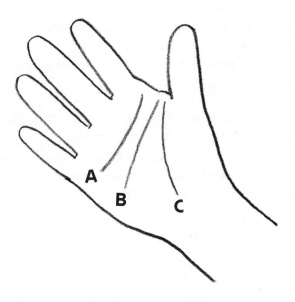

Mystery Night

Collecting clues and solving mysteries make for an excellent family night. There are plenty of activities in this section, and you can enhance Mystery Night by playing board games such as Clue and Clue Junior. You can even rent the fun movie named *Clue*, which is based on the board game.

Mystery Night is also a great time to read mystery stories, like the Nancy Drew Mystery series and The Hardy Boys mysteries. There are mysterious treats to eat and many mysteries to solve, so get out your magnifying glass and quote Sherlock Holmes by saying, "Elementary, my dear Watson, elementary!"

Secret Codes

Create a secret code and write notes to each other. See if others can break the code and figure out your message. Here are some examples of secret codes you can use:

❋ Write the next letter in the alphabet for each letter you are writing. "Dear Dad" would read "Efbs Ebe."

❋ Use the same code as above, only write the next consonant for consonants and the next vowel for vowels. "Dear Mom" would read "Fies Nun."

❋ Write backward. "Dear Sister" would read "Raed Retsis."

Sir Arthur Conan Doyle wrote four novels and 56 short stories about Sherlock Holmes.

Two-Minute Mysteries

Agatha Christie, a famous mystery writer, wrote a lot about poisons, which she learned about while she worked in a hospital during World War I.

You can get books of two-minute mysteries from the library. They are great fun to share with the family. The way it works is one family member reads the mystery and the answer to the mystery to himself or herself. That person then reads the mystery only (not the answer) out loud to the rest of the family. Other family members may ask yes or no questions as they work together to solve the mystery. Here is an example of my favorite two-minute mystery:

Mystery: George and Martha were found lying dead in the living room. There was glass and water everywhere. What happened?

Answer: George and Martha are fish. Their fish tank broke.

Here's another good one:

Mystery: A man and his son were in a car accident. The man died, and his son was rushed to the hospital. While in surgery the doctor said, "I cannot operate on this boy. He is my son." How is that possible?

Answer: The surgeon is his mother.

Bang Bang

This activity, and the next two (Crossed/Uncrossed and I'm Going to a Party), are all games where you try to figure out what the rule is. Once you know the rule, you can make changes to it, so you can keep playing different versions of these games.

For this game you pantomime (that is, you do the motions while pretending) shooting a gun. Making a shooting motion with your hand, you say, "Bang, bang, bang. Who'd I shoot?" The other family members have to figure out who you shot. The rule is that the first person to speak after you say, "Who'd I shoot?" is the one who got shot.

Take turns shooting people. You can say, "bang" as many times as you want, and point in any direction. It doesn't matter, because the rule has nothing to do with that. It only depends on who speaks when you are done.

Even people who haven't figured out the rule yet can have a turn shooting. It's funny when they don't understand how they shot someone.

Edgar Allen Poe is credited with creating the detective story.

Crossed/Uncrossed

What You Need

❋ 2 spoons

1. All family members should sit in a circle.
2. Holding the two spoons any way you like, hand them to the person next to you saying, "crossed" or "uncrossed." One of them is correct based on the rule.
3. Continue taking turns passing the spoons in the circle, saying "crossed" or "uncrossed," and let the other family members know if they are correct based on the rule.
4. The rule: "Crossed" and "uncrossed" refers to your legs, not the spoons. If your legs are crossed, "crossed" is the right answer, even if the spoons are uncrossed.

Nancy Drew mystery books are known around the world and have been translated into at least 14 different languages.

I'm Going to a Party

Everyone takes turns saying "I'm going to a party, and I'm going to wear . . . "and each person finishes the sentence with an item of clothing they plan to wear to a party. You tell them whether or not they can go, based on the rule. You can play this game over and over again with different rules each time. Here are some ideas for rules:

1. You say you will wear something that the person on your left is wearing.
2. You say you will wear something that a designated family member is wearing.
3. You say you will wear something that starts with the same letter as your name.
4. You say you will wear something that has double letters in it, such as zippers.
5. You say you will wear something that starts with the last letter of the previous thing that was said.

> The term "unravel the clue" comes from the fact that the word *clue* originally meant a ball of thread.

 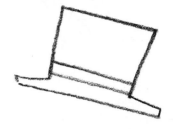

Here's an example of the first rule listed above:

Josh, Barbara, J.R., Amy, and Diego are sitting in a circle. Josh makes up the rule.

Josh says, "I'm going to a party, and I'm going to wear green pants. I can go." (He can go because Barbara, who is sitting to Josh's left, is wearing green pants.)

Barbara says, "I'm going to a party, and I'm going to wear a dress." Josh tells Barbara she cannot go, but does not tell her that the reason is because J.R., who is sitting to her left, is not wearing a dress.

J.R. says, "I'm going to a party, and I'm going to wear a hat." Josh tells J.R. he cannot go, but does not tell him that the reason is because Amy, who is sitting to J.R.'s left, is not wearing a hat.

Amy says, "I'm going to a party, and I'm going to wear a T-shirt." Josh tells Amy she can go, but Amy may not know that the reason is because Diego, who is sitting to Amy's left, is wearing a T-shirt. The game continues until everyone has figured out why he or she can or cannot go to the party.

Cross-Examination

One family member plays the detective in this activity. Once chosen, the detective must leave the room. The remaining family members must decide which person will be the guilty party.

Bring the detective back into the room. The detective asks one question, such as, "Where were you the night the cookies disappeared?" Each family member makes up an answer and tells the detective. Then the detective asks the same question again. Each family member restates his or her answer. The guilty person changes his story slightly.

See if the detective can catch the guilty person by listening carefully to his statement and noticing the change.

Here's an example of how this game is played:

Mom is the detective and leaves the room. Leigh Anna is chosen to be the guilty person.

Mom returns and asks, "What were you doing when the rabbit disappeared from the hat?" J.R. says, "I was eating popcorn in the den." Dad says, "I was sleeping with the cat on my lap." Leigh Anna says, "I was reading a book titled *How the West Was Lost*." Josh says, "I was making Swedish meatballs in the kitchen."

Mom asks, "Could you please tell me once again what you were doing when the rabbit disappeared?" Everyone repeats his or her story the same way except for Leigh Anna, who replies, "I was reading a book titled *How the West Was Won*."

Will Mom detect Leigh Anna is guilty based on the book title change?

The Hardy Boys and Nancy Drew have solved mysteries on all seven continents!

Guess the Flavor

Detectives must use all of their senses when solving crimes. In this game you must use your sense of taste.

What You Need

❋ A blindfold (a scarf works well)

❋ Food that comes in different flavors such as fruit-flavored cereal or fruit-flavored candy, like jellybeans

1. Blindfold one member of the family.

2. Have the blindfolded person open her mouth and carefully place one of the candies in her mouth. Or you can put the candy in her hand, and then she will put the candy in her own mouth.

3. See if the blindfolded person can guess what color and flavor she is eating.

Fingerprints

Fingerprints are very interesting. In ancient Babylon, fingerprints on clay tablets were used for business transactions. Ancient Chinese seals feature thumbprints. In the 14th century a doctor discovered that no two fingerprints are exactly alike. In 1880 a doctor named Faulds first discussed the possibility of using fingerprints as a means of identification. In 1883 Mark Twain wrote a book titled Life on the Mississippi *that contains the story of a murderer who was identified in court by his fingerprints. The police began to use the fingerprint system in 1891.*

What You Need

❋ Inkpad

❋ Paper

❋ Markers (optional)

1. Take your fingerprint by pressing the tip of your finger into the ink pad, then pressing it down on a piece of paper.

2. Have other members of the family take their fingerprints, too.

3. See how your fingerprint compares with the fingerprints of other members of your family.

If you're looking for a craft activity for Mystery Night, try creating fingerprint art. Use your fingerprint as the body of animals, snowmen, or other things. Use markers to draw the rest of the objects around the fingerprints. This creates a unique, one-of-a-kind piece of art, because nobody else has your fingerprint.

> Birds have three fingers under their wings, but they don't have fingerprints.

Solve the (Pillow) Case

In this activity you need to use your sense of touch to figure out clues.

What You Need

❋ An empty pillowcase

❋ A variety of dissimilar objects, such as a teddy bear, calculator, shoe, gravy ladle, back scratcher, and hairbrush

1. Out of sight of the other family members, put an object inside the pillowcase.

2. Then pass the pillowcase around to the others and see who can guess what the object is without looking.

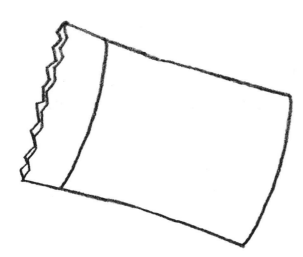

Detective Wink

What You Need

❋ Deck of cards

1. Remove from the deck the ace of spades and enough cards to equal one for each family member (including the ace).

2. Shuffle those cards and deal them out.

3. Each person should look at his or her card but not let anyone else see it. The person who has the ace of spades is the killer. Everyone looks around, being sure to make eye contact. If the killer wants to kill someone, she winks at the person while the other person is looking.

4. If you have been winked at, wait 10 seconds, then lie down "dead." Once one person has died, another family member can try to guess who the killer is. If that person guesses wrong, he or she must also "die." If he or she guesses right, that person wins the game. You cannot make a guess if you are already "dead."

> The iris in the human eye is an even better means of identification than a fingerprint.

99

I Spy

One of my family's favorite pass-the-time games is I Spy. I'll say, "I spy, with my little eye, something" and a color. The other family members then have to guess what object I am thinking of based on the color. The object must be something within sight of where the game is played.

The I Spy books and computer games are great for the entire family. They are filled with collages of things to find—some easy, some difficult.

For a fun craft and family game, create your own I Spy collage.

What You Need

* Scissors
* Magazines
* Construction paper
* Glue
* Pen
* Paper
* A grown-up to assist

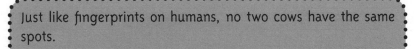

Just like fingerprints on humans, no two cows have the same spots.

1. Cut out a lot of different pictures from magazines and glue them onto the construction paper, creating a collage. Use all different things, of all different sizes. You can create a theme for your collage and all pictures must be related to this theme. Here are some suggestions for themes:

* Underwater	* Toy box
* Sky	* Laboratory
* Haunted house	* Jungle
* Garden	

2. After you have made your collage, make a list of items for your family to find.

3. Exchange your collage with another family member and find the objects in each other's pictures.

Scrapbook Night

Not only is this an enjoyable family night, it results in treasures that family members will enjoy for generations to come. In addition to working on your current scrapbook, take some time on Scrapbook Night to look through old photo albums together. Tell each other about the memories and the people pictured in the photographs.

If you enjoy creating scrapbooks, you can take classes at scrapbook stores such as Archiver's or through companies such as Creative Memories. You can also transfer your photographs onto video or CD and set them to music. This makes a beautiful keepsake for you and your family, or a nice presentation at a wedding or family reunion.

Regardless of what you choose to do with your photographs, enjoy them and treasure them, along with your great memories.

Family Pages

What You Need

* A scrapbook or photo album

* Photographs and other mementos such as postcards

* Scissors

* Corner cutters (optional; available at scrapbook or craft stores)

* Stickers, colored paper, stencils to decorate (optional)

* Adhesive made especially for photos

* Markers, various colors

* A grown-up to assist

Putting your photographs into a scrapbook—selecting the ones to include, organizing them, and simply starting the project—can be overwhelming. Making it a family activity is a great way to get it done while having fun and sharing memories. If you feel like you have so many photographs and don't know where to begin, start small, choose a theme or format, and just do it. Creating a scrapbook of at least a portion of your photographs is better than none at all, and, as one of my scrapbook teachers told me once when I was struggling to make a perfect page, "Done is better than perfect."

Here are some ideas for themes and formats:

* Choose a family vacation and divide it by days. Create a page in a scrapbook for each day of the trip.

* Choose a holiday and gather all of the photographs from that holiday, regardless of the year.

* Make an alphabet book. Put pictures of memories that begin with each letter of the alphabet.

* Divide your photographs by season, regardless of the year.

* Make a birthday book.

* Make different pages for each family member. Mix up the order of the pages in the book so you can keep adding to it in any order as the book continues.

* Choose a theme for your book such as sports, parties, good times, laughter, dance, celebrations, or the great outdoors.

Here are the basic steps to creating a scrapbook.

1. Choose the photographs you want to use. Organize your photographs by theme, date, or however you choose. Select four to six photographs to go on one page together.

2. Crop your photographs. Decide how best to crop each photograph. You can trim the edges so that the subject is centered; that way you don't waste room in your scrapbook with background you don't need. You can use a corner cutter to round the corners of your photographs and give them a nice, professional look. (Fancy corner cutters give pictures a lacey outline.)

3. You can cut a shape around the subject of the photo, such as a heart, oval, or star. You can also trim closely around the subject of the photograph like a paper doll.

4. Arrange the photos on your scrapbook pages.

5. Glue the photos to the page with the adhesive.

6. Choose and arrange embellishments such as stickers or borders of pretty paper.

7. Write captions or other notes with the markers.

You may only get one or two pages done in your scrapbook on Scrapbook Night. That's OK—you can continue the next time.

Stamping

Stamping is a great way to embellish your scrapbook or to create unique greeting cards and invitations. Here's an example of how to create a greeting card and a little gift all in one! You can make the card and gift or just have fun creating art with your stamps.

What You Need

* Paper or light cardboard
* Ink pad
* Ribbon
* Markers or pencils, optional
* Scissors
* Stamps
* A grown-up to assist

1. Cut out a piece of light cardboard or construction paper about one inch wide and four inches long. This will become a bookmark.
2. Cut a small hole at the top and in the center of the bookmark.
3. Decorate the bookmark with your stamps.
4. Tie ribbon through the hole in the top of the bookmark.
5. Fold another piece of light cardboard in half to create your card.
6. Cut two horizontal slits in the front of the card, about two inches apart, and a little more than one inch long.
7. Decorate the card with your stamps.
8. Slide the bookmark through the slits in the front of the card.

After stamping, you can color in the stamp with colored markers or pencils to add color to your creation.

Journal Details

Have you ever looked through an old photo album and wondered who everybody is or what year it was? It may seem hard to imagine, but someday that will happen with your scrapbook. That's why journaling is so very important.

Leave room on every page of your scrapbook to write a little description about the page and the photographs. Here are some suggestions:

* Names of people in the photographs
* Places the photographs were taken
* Dates the photographs were taken, or at least the year
* Special memories
* Quotes from people in the photographs

Alphabet Book

This is a special book for a young member of your family, or a gift your family can work on together to give to a new baby.

What You Need

* Camera
* Scrapbook with 26 pages, or light cardboard to become the pages in the book
* Colored markers
* Glue
* Scissors
* A grown-up to assist

1. Use the camera to take pictures of things that begin with each letter of the alphabet. Make some of the items personal and special to the person who will be receiving the book; for example, take pictures of family members or favorite blankets and stuffed animals. You may want to take the pictures in advance, get them developed or printed, and have them ready to put into the book on Scrapbook Night.

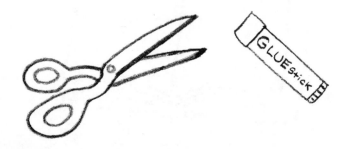

Here are some ideas:

A	aunt, apple	**M**	mom, mouse
B	baby, brother, blanket, bottle	**N**	nose, nap
		O	owl, orange
C	cookie, cat	**P**	peanut butter, papa
D	dad, dog	**Q**	queen, quilt
E	elephant, egg	**R**	rock, raisin
F	friend, feather	**S**	smile, snake, sister
G	grandma, grandpa, grapes	**T**	teacher, turtle
		U	uncle, umbrella
H	hand, horse, hug	**V**	violin
I	ice cream	**W**	wave, wet
J	jelly	**X**	X-ray, xylophone
K	kitten, ketchup	**Y**	yard, yogurt
L	lion, lollipop	**Z**	zebra

2. Create a page for each letter of the alphabet. Use the markers to write or stencil the letter on each page.

3. Glue the picture of the object that starts with that letter onto the page.

4. Decorate the page with fun shapes, drawings, or cutouts from magazines of other things that start with the letter.

5. Be sure to write the name of the recipient and the name of the person who made the book at the beginning or end of the book.

Shapes and Sizes

If you are looking for a simple way to decorate your scrapbook or create a collage, you might try shapes.

What You Need

* Colored paper
* Scissors
* Glue
* A grown-up to assist

1. Cut out different sizes of shapes with different-colored paper. Here are some ideas:

   * Stars
   * Triangles
   * Circles
   * Ovals
   * Hearts
   * Squares
   * Flowers
   * Rectangles
   * Long strips of paper of different widths

2. Use the shapes to decorate a scrapbook or to create a collage. Use your imagination! Here are some suggestions:

   * Make borders with the strips, and glue smaller shapes on top of the strips.
   * Put larger shapes in each corner, and smaller ones on top of those.
   * Use circles and ovals to make thought bubbles and comic book–type quotes that people in the pictures might be thinking or are saying.
   * Put small shapes in the corners of the photos to create a sort of frame.
   * Disperse many sizes of the same shape throughout the scrapbook page to create a mood, such as bright-colored flowers for a spring look, fall colors for a seasonal look, or hearts for a romantic look.

Family History Night

This night can be done in conjunction with *Scrapbook Night* or as a night by itself. It's a great way to share valuable stories and realize how you are connected to everyone in your family.

It is important to learn about your family, your ancestors, and their experiences and stories. You can learn how your ancestors were similar to and different from you, and how living conditions and education have changed over time. There's a board game called *Life Stories* that you can play on this night. In this game you receive story cards as you travel around the board. The cards are divided into such categories as past experiences, influences, and future plans. You answer different questions, or tell different stories, depending on where you land. This chapter also has many activities that will help you create your own family games.

Family Portraits

Imagine that your family is posing for a portrait. In this portrait you want to portray something about each family member, show his or her relationship to everyone else in the family, and show something about the family as a whole.

Choose one family member to be the photographer. This person tells everyone else how to pose for the portrait. This person positions family members in a way that communicates something about each person. After the photographer has posed every other family member, he should tell the others why he posed them as he did. The photographer should also talk about what he tried to show in the picture. This might lead to some interesting family discussions!

Here are some examples of poses:

❋ If you feel that the entire family revolves around your little sister, put her in the middle, perhaps up high on a stool, and have everyone else stand around her. Some family members may be smiling; others may not.

❋ You may choose to show each family member pretending to be involved in their favorite hobby, or something they do a lot. Perhaps one child is kicking a ball, a parent is on the phone, another child is on the computer, and the other parent is reading the paper.

❋ Your parents can make a family portrait reflecting the families they grew up in. Use current family members to play the grandparents, uncles, or aunts who may have grown up in the home with your mom or dad. See what you can learn about what their lives were like.

❋ For funny portraits, the photographer can call out different silly kinds of families and have everyone pose like those families. Examples include a family of nerds, a sleepy family, a family of spies, a musical family, or a gross family.

If you like, take pictures of your family in the portraits, and turn the pictures into a family collage.

Life Stories

What You Need

* Index cards, at least four for each family member
* Pens

1. On each index card each person should write one question or the beginning of a story. Here are some ideas:

   * What talent did you inherit from your grandmother?
   * Once there was an athlete in my family and . . .
   * If you could, what is one question you wish you had asked a relative before he or she died?
   * The weirdest neighbor I ever had . . .
   * Once a relative did an embarrassing thing . . .
   * My mom or dad always said it was important to . . .
   * A very memorable dinner was when . . .
   * My mom or dad was very happy when . . .
   * When I grow up I want to be _____ because . . . (for kids)
   * I decided to work as a _____ because . . . (for adults)
   * I'm a lot like my aunt (or another relative) because . . .
   * When it's hot outside, my favorite thing to do with my family is . . .
   * When it's cold outside, my favorite thing to do with my family is . . .
   * How did you learn your manners?
   * Once I received flowers because . . .
   * The strangest job one of my relatives ever had was as a . . .

   In many African nations people hold initiation ceremonies for groups of children instead of birthdays. When children reach a certain age they learn the laws, beliefs, customs, or songs and dances of their tribe.

   * What was your childhood best friend like?
   * Did you ever use an unusual form of transportation?
   * Describe a memorable event in school (or from school days, if you are out of school).
   * Do you have a favorite fashion trend?
   * What has been invented in your lifetime?
   * I have an old photograph from . . .
   * Describe a time you were sick, and how you got better.
   * Describe the place you grew up.
   * One time I felt like a fish out of water when . . .
   * I once experienced another culture when I went to _____ and did this:
   * Did you ever play a joke on someone?
   * My hero is . . .
   * Describe a favorite book or story.
   * Is there a friend or relative you'd like to see again soon?
   * Once I met someone famous . . .
   * Describe a time when you moved.
   * Do you have a favorite family restaurant?
   * What states or countries are your grandparents from?

* One time I got into trouble at school because . . .

* What was your favorite childhood game?

* What are your hobbies?

* Have you ever been in an accident?

* Have you ever been to a funeral?

* Have you ever been in a wedding?

* One day, when I went swimming . . .

* What is your favorite car trip game or song?

* What musical instrument is played in your family?

* What early television show do you remember?

* How did you meet someone important in your life? (spouse, best friend)

* Describe a time when it was just you and one other family member.

2. Have everyone sit in a circle.

3. One person collects and shuffles the index cards, and deals them out so that each family member gets four.

4. Each person should take a few minutes to look at his or her cards, read them, and decide which one to talk about.

5. Take turns telling stories based on the cards you were dealt. If you'd rather, you can write about the stories and then read them aloud to each other.

Oral Histories

Interview the people in your immediate family, and then interview your relatives. Videotape or record the conversations. The recordings will become a part of your family's history. Here are some topics to bring up as you interview your subject:

* The first and last name of every great grandparent, uncle, aunt, and cousin you can remember

* Places you lived and how you arrived there

* Where you went to school

* How you met your husband or wife

* History and war stories

* Special family vacations

* Items you own that have sentimental or financial value, and how you came to have each item

* What you remember about the day your children were born

* How you chose your children's names

* How you chose your occupation

Time Capsule

This is a fun activity for now and will be again in years to come.

What You Need

❉ Tin or metal box with a lid that seals

❉ Paper

❉ Pens

❉ Materials that you collect (see below for ideas)

1. Decide when you will open your time capsule—in 1 year? In 10 years? In 20 years?
2. Gather materials that will be interesting in the future.
3. Put everything in the capsule, seal it, and label it with the words, "Do not open until (date you have chosen)." Here are

---

ideas for things to place inside your time capsule:

❉ Photographs

❉ Newspaper clippings

❉ Menus from your favorite restaurants

❉ A list of today's prices for things such as gas, milk, and a movie

❉ The names of top film stars and actors

❉ The name of the president

❉ Hit songs and popular bands

❉ Pages from a current fashion magazine

❉ The name of the teams that won popular sports events such as the Super Bowl or the World Series

❉ Predictions for the future

❉ Secret notes to other members of the family, not to be read until the capsule is opened

---

Have you heard of the wedding expression "something old, something new, something borrowed, and something blue"? Here's what it means:

❉ Something old represents a gift from the bride's family as a token to remember her premarried life.

❉ Something new represents happiness for the new family being formed.

❉ Something borrowed represents something from another happily married person, so the happiness will continue.

❉ Something blue represents purity.

Trains, Planes, and Automobiles Night

The sights and sounds of trains, airplanes, and cars have always excited kids, and even some adults. Train toys, collectibles, and museums are just some things that show our fascination with railroads. Taking flight is always exciting, and the thought of humans flying like birds has enticed humans through time. Airplanes come in many shapes and sizes, and are interesting to study. And people love cars. Families spend a lot of time with each other in their car; some even attend car shows together. Trains, Planes, and Automobiles Night will rev up your family in a really fun way.

Racecar

Here's a fun game that requires no props or set up; it just requires everyone to pay attention and to work together. With the family sitting in a circle, imagine that you have a pretend racecar in your hands. Set the imaginary racecar down in front of you. Next, push it toward the family member on your left, and say "zoom." That family member drives it on to his or her left by saying "zoom" and making a pushing motion toward the left, or says one of the following:

Screech! Saying "screech!" stops the racecar. If you say "screech!", you may then say "zoom" in the opposite direction. When you say "screech!" put your hand out as if to say "stop."

Pit stop! Saying "pit stop" makes the car skip the next player in the circle. Put your hands out in front of you, over the imaginary racecar, when you say "pit stop."

Oil slick! Saying "oil slick" changes the direction of the racecar and skips the next player in the new direction. Move your finger in a circle when you say "oil slick."

You can play this game for fun or for elimination. If you play for elimination, here are the ways that someone is eliminated:

※ If a player doesn't follow the directions
※ If a player misses the direction of the car after an oil slick or pit stop
※ If a player reverses direction without saying "screech!"
※ If player pauses too long

The player who is eliminated leaves the circle. The game continues until only one player is left.

Hula Hoop Game

Have some fun with hula hoops. Use them to create unusual planes, trains, and automobiles. See how many different ways you can use them, and how many different body parts can spin them and balance them.

What You Need

※ Hula hoops   ※ Fun music (optional)

1. Pass a hula hoop around and see how many different ways you can use it. Use your imagination to think of different things a hula hoop can be. Use the hula hoop in an unusual way and see if other family members can guess what you are using it for. Here are some suggestions:

   ※ Steering wheel   ※ Rings of Saturn
   ※ Angel halo   ※ Necklace
   ※ Life preserver

2. You can also bounce the hula hoop or tap it on the floor. You can crawl through it like a circus performer.

3. If the hula hoop is big enough, or you are small enough, you can jump rope with the hula hoop. Hold it in front of you with both hands. Jump through it, then lift it up your back, over your head, and jump through it again.

4. Have hula hoop contests. Put on some fun music and bounce the hoops, jump rope, or use the hula hoops in the traditional way. See which family members can last the longest.

Family 500

This event is named for the Indianapolis 500.

What You Need

* All of the toy cars in your home
* Cardboard, a long piece
* Several books

1. Bring all the toy cars into one room. Take turns choosing cars until each one is selected.

2. Make a ramp out of the long piece of cardboard and piles of books. (You might need to hold the ramp steady.)

3. Two family members race one car each for each race. The first car down the ramp is the winner. The winning car of each race goes back to its player; the other is eliminated.

4. Continue racing all the cars in this way, alternating players and cars until finally you have two players and two cars left. The winner of this final race is the _____ (insert your family name here) Family 500 winner!

Driving Tempo

Here's a way to have musical fun while actively using your imagination. Turn your home into a busy street. Put on some slow music, such as "I've Been Working on the Railroad" or "Leaving on a Jet Plane," and everyone becomes a slow car. Then put on fast music, such as "Come on Baby, Do the Locomotion" or "Little Red Caboose," and see everyone drive fast. You can choose to be a particular type of car. If you decide to be a luxury car, you might want to lean back and look important while you "drive" around your house. Or if you choose to be an economy car, then maybe move around the house as if you're all squished up and beep your high-pitched horn as you drive.

Once everyone's car has run out of gas, try being another form of transportation such as a train. If each person becomes a train, you can even hook your arms together, like train cars, or move your arms around the way a train wheel moves. See if you can make the train go fast and slow. What kind of train are you? Are you part of a circus train? Or are you carrying sugar, corn, lumber, or maybe even cars? You can also become airplanes, "flying" around your house together. While you're making airplane noises be sure to take time to look at the scenery. Try and imagine seeing a river or mountains or even a baseball field below as you fly high up in the sky—your imagination is the only ticket you need.

Wheels on the Car

In this activity you make up your own song similar to the "Wheels on the Bus" song.

Think of all the parts of a car or a plane or a train. Change the words to this well-known song and sing it together. Here's some help to begin the sing-along fun:

Of course the wheels on the car go round and round
And the horn on the car goes beep, beep, beep
And the wipers on the car go swish, swish, swish

But how about:

The kids in the car say, "Are we there yet?"
The radio in the car sings, "La, la, la"
The seatbelts in the car go "Click, click, click"
The lights in the car go off and on
The engine in the car goes rrrr, rrrr, rrrrr
The windows in the car go up and down

What other sounds does a car make? You make up more lyrics for these sounds.

You can also make up a song about a plane trip:

The flight attendant on the plane says, "Seat belts on"
The seats on the plane go up and back
The trays on the plane go up and down
The pilot on the plane says, "Thanks for flying"
The babies on the plane go "Wah, wah, wah" (crying)
The snacks on the plane are yum, yum, yum

And how about a song for the train:

The conductor on the train yells, "All aboard!"
The whistle on the train goes wooo, wooo, wooo
The wheels on the train go chug, chug, chug

You can sing these lyrics, make up your own, or think of another form of transportation, such as a bike, for creating a new song.

You can make up hand movements for each line in your song, too.

Scavenger Hunt Night

For this family night, you will have to set up some things in advance. You also need to choose one family member to lead the activities. For most of these activities you have to hide the clues around the house so that each one leads to the next.

You can use scavenger hunts in conjunction with Mystery Night or with holiday and birthday celebrations—just adjust the theme of the hunt accordingly. Whichever scavenger hunt activities you choose, your family is sure to enjoy the thrill of the hunt.

Each Other Trivia

What You Need

* Pieces of paper

* Pen

* Tape

For an Each Other Trivia scavenger hunt, come up with questions about items in your house that are significant to family members. Here are some examples:

* This picture is of Dad's favorite place.

* This is Mom's favorite food.

* Aidan brought home this souvenir from our last vacation.

* This item used to belong to Grandma.

1. You'll need about 20 items for this list. Write each one down on a separate piece of paper.

2. Number them, leaving out number 1.

3. Tape number 2 to the answer to number 1; tape number 3 to the answer to number 2, and so on. That way each item you find will have a clue that will lead you to the next item. That way each clue leads to the next.

4. When your family is ready to play the game, give them clue number 1 and start the hunt!

Around the House Trivia

Come up with trivia questions about household items. You can use the Internet to find out who invented different appliances, or what year they were invented, and convert that information into the form of a question.

Use the same system as in Each Other Trivia—tape the clues to the answers so that each answer leads to the next clue. Here are a few of my favorite Around the House Trivia questions and answers.

Question: This was invented by Alexander Graham Bell.
Answer: The telephone.

Question: We never look here on Sundays.
Answer: The mailbox.

Question: When this was first invented, it was five and a half feet tall.
Answer: The microwave oven.

Question: This musical instrument was inspired by a hunting bow.
Answer: The harp.

If You Want to Find a . . .

Younger family members will have fun creating this scavenger hunt for the rest of the family. This scavenger hunt leads family members all over the house before they find the hidden object.

What You Need

* Paper
* Pen
* Something to hide, such as a teddy bear

1. Write the first clue: "If you want to find the teddy bear (or whatever your hidden object is), go to the dollhouse."
2. At the dollhouse leave another clue: "Then go to the linen closet."
3. At the linen closet leave another clue: "Next, go to the fruit bowl."
4. At the fruit bowl leave the clue: "Now look under Mom and Dad's bed." There's where the teddy bear is! Let each person in the family have a chance to pick an object and write and hide the clues.

Do people eat Easter eggs once they find them? Yes, at least 64 percent of people do.

Silly Scavenger Hunt

This kind of scavenger hunt requires more physical activity than the others and can be as silly as you want.

What You Need

* Paper
* Pens or pencils
* A list of 10 to 20 funny tasks family members must do

1. You can begin this activity with each family member making up a unique list of activities or silly actions to do. Or one person can provide the list and then every family member reorders the activities. Or you can divide into two teams and have each team provide the list for the other team.
2. The family members or teams start in the same room. After they've completed all of their tasks, they return to the starting place. The first family member or team to return wins.

Here are some ideas for tasks:

* Say "meow" 10 times while petting the cat.
* Put on another person's winter coat and zip it all the way up.
* Tie your shoelaces together and try to walk from the living room to the kitchen.
* Sing "Twinkle, Twinkle, Little Star" while staring out the highest window in your house.
* Stand in the bathtub and pretend to wash your hair.
* Do five jumping jacks in the dining room.
* Put on lipstick and kiss a mirror.
* Put on a necktie and tie it the right way.
* Do the chicken dance with a pair of socks on your hands.

At the Mall

While most of the activities in this book are intended for family fun at home, here is one outside-the-home activity—a scavenger hunt at the shopping mall. It's important to have an adult on each team, and all team members must stay together for safety.

What You Need

* Pens

* Paper

* Money (Each adult team member should have a small amount of money, such as $5, to spend during the hunt for these items.)

1. Divide your family into teams, with an adult on each team.
2. Each team takes a copy of the following list.
3. Decide on a meeting place. The first team to return to the meeting place with everything on the list wins.

OK, ready, set, here's the list:

* Autograph from a makeup counter worker who applied make-up to one team member

* Catalog

* Business card, from someone working in the mall or someone shopping

* Candy

* Piece of nylon, available in shoe departments for free (for trying on a pair of shoes)

* Something a talking toy says in a toy store, written on a piece of paper

* The cost of the most expensive item in a jewelry store and what it is, written on a piece of paper

* Cup

* Little brown bag

* Toy

* Something that smells

* Something purple

* Something glittery

* Something mushy

* Something cute

* Something that makes noise

* Bookmark

* Napkin signed by a food court employee

This list is just a suggestion. You can create your own list together.

Scavenging for Lyrics

Turn song lyrics into the clues for your scavenger hunt.

What You Need

❋ Paper

❋ Pens

❋ Tape

1. Think of songs that have household objects or places mentioned in the lyrics. Write the lines from the songs, leaving the clue word blank, on separate sheets of paper. For an extra clue, you can tell the players what songs the lines are from, but you don't have to.

2. Using the same system as in Each Other Trivia, tape the clues so that each clue leads to the next.

Here are some ideas for song lyric clues:

❋ *Buy me some _____ and crackerjack* from "Take Me Out to the Ball Game." (Hide the next clue with some peanuts.)

❋ *Splish, splash, I was taking a _____* from "Splish Splash." (Hide the next clue in the bathtub.)

❋ *Bright copper kettles and warm woolen _____* from "My Favorite Things" from the movie *The Sound of Music*. (Hide the clue in a pair of mittens.)

❋ *Try the gray stuff. It's delicious! You don't believe me? Ask the _____* from the song "Be Our Guest" from the movie *Beauty and the Beast*. (Hide the clue with the dishes.)

> There were 52 musicians in composer Johann Sebastian Bach's family. Musical talent definitely runs in the family.

Winter in July Night

On a hot summer night it's fun to cool off and imagine it's wintertime. If you love wintertime it can be hard to go all summer long without fun wintertime activities. Why wait? Use your imagination and pretend. Make marshmallow snowmen, and let them melt in your hot chocolate. Watch *A Charlie Brown Christmas* and any other holiday videos you may have. Put on your cozy slippers and maybe even your stocking cap. Gather around the fireplace (real or pretend) and share your favorite wintertime memories. Put on your mittens and enjoy a cozy winter day in the middle of July!

Wintery Songs

Have a winter song sing-along to celebrate the magic of the season and the holidays at this time of year. If you have bells, then jingle them while you sing. Or use the lids of pots to make cymbals or an upside-down wastepaper basket to beat out a rhythm to help keep time while you sing. Here are some songs to celebrate this season, even when it's too hot to play outside:

* "Walking in a Winter Wonderland" (If you don't know the lyrics, type the title within quotation marks into your favorite Internet search engine to find these online.)
* "Heat Miser/Snow Miser"
* "Jingle Bells"
* "Suzy Snowflake"
* "Rudolph the Red-Nosed Reindeer"
* "Let It Snow"
* "Frosty the Snowman"

You can also make up your own lyrics to well-known songs such as "The Twelve Days of Christmas." You can change this song to "The Twelve Days of Winter." Family members can take turns making up new lines: "On the first day of winter, my true love gave to me . . ." They finish the line with something they'd like to have such as "A cool outfit for my Barbie." Another family member follows by singing: "On the second day of winter, my true love gave to me . . ." and finishing the line with something original like "Two slices of pizza." And everyone sings: "And a cool outfit for my Barbie," just as in the traditional version. Continue the song taking turns adding new lyrics until you have sung all 12 days.

Candy Houses

In my family, we don't actually eat this creation. We leave it out for a few weeks as a great-smelling centerpiece.

What You Need

* Cookie sheet or box top
* Marshmallow fluff
* Pound cake
* White frosting
* Spatula
* Graham crackers or wafer cookies to be the roof
* Variety of candies such as candy-coated chocolates, gumdrops, and hard candies

1. Cover the cookie sheet or box top with marshmallow fluff to create snow.
2. Place the pound cake in the middle of the snow.
3. Cover the cake with the white frosting using the spatula.
4. Create a roof with crackers and/or cookies. Use more marshmallow fluff to affix.
5. Decorate the house with candies.

This is completely edible but you might just want to look at it, too.

> A family in Brussels, Belgium, founded Godiva chocolates in 1926.

Candy Cane Sugar Cookies

The smell and taste of these will bring you back to wintertime.

What You Need

* Teaspoon
* Measuring cup
* Water
* Red sprinkles or icing
* Refrigerated tube of precut sugar cookies
* Cookie sheet
* Powdered sugar
* Small bowl
* Knife
* A grown-up to assist

1. Preheat the oven according to directions on the refrigerated tube of cookie dough.
2. Take a rounded teaspoonful of cookie dough and roll it into a worm. (Ignore the precut marks in the dough.)
3. Shape the worm into a candy cane and place on an ungreased cookie sheet. You can fit about 8 to 12 candy canes on the cookie sheet at once. Make sure to spread them out because they will become wider as they bake.
4. Bake according to the directions on cookie dough package.
5. Let the cookies cool.
6. Place about a cup of powdered sugar into a small bowl.
7. Add about a teaspoon of water to the powdered sugar and mix thoroughly.
8. Continue adding water until the mixture is the consistency of icing.
9. Use a knife to spread the icing over the cookies.
10. Use red sprinkles to make stripes across the candy canes. Now enjoy them!

Reindeer Food

Why should the humans have all the treats? Don't forget that it's the season for flying reindeer! They'll need magic food. Here's the recipe:

What You Need

* Oats, uncooked
* Glitter

1. Combine the oats and the glitter.
2. Go outside and try to throw the reindeer food onto the roof of your house. See how the food sparkles in the air. You can tell it's magical, and helps the reindeer fly!

The magical film *Fantasia* was the first to use stereophonic sound.

Grab Bag Gift Giving

This may not be a traditional season for gift giving, but giving is always a joy. So play this grab bag game that will have the entire family giving and grabbing!

What You Need

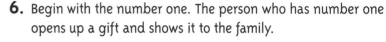

* Gifts (see below for ideas)
* Wrapping paper
* Clear tape
* Scissors
* Small pieces of paper
* Pen
* Hat or bowl
* A grown-up to assist

1. Everyone finds one or more items of their own to give in this activity. (The more things you bring to give, the more you'll get.) You can select something that is yours and that you no longer want, something you made, or something you bought.

2. Privately wrap each gift so no one else sees the gift before it's wrapped. Place all the wrapped gifts in the center of one room.

3. Count the number of gifts. Write down numbers beginning with the number one on each slip of paper, and continue until you reach the total number of wrapped gifts.

4. Fold up each piece of paper and place it in the hat or bowl.

5. Without looking, each family member chooses numbers from the bowl. Choose one number for each gift you wrapped and brought to this activity.

6. Begin with the number one. The person who has number one opens up a gift and shows it to the family.

7. The person who drew number two goes next. This person has two choices: She can take number one's gift, or open another one. If she chooses to take number one's gift, then number one gets to open another gift. If she chooses to open a new gift, then after unwrapping it she shows it to the rest of the family.

8. Now it's number three's turn. Number three can take number one's gift, number two's gift, or open an unopened gift. If number three takes the gift from number one, then number one can take number two's gift or open a new gift, and so on.

9. Continue the game until all gifts have been opened.

Here are some rules to help this game along:

* You cannot take back something that was just taken from you. You may, however, take it back on another turn.

* An object cannot be taken more than once per turn.

Blanket Sleds

You can go sledding in your house and pretend you are sledding on snow in winter. Drag your brother or sister—or even Mom or Dad—around the house on a blanket. If you have carpeted stairs, work with your parents to make this a safe sledding experience, too. Here are some ideas for making this activity even more exciting:

❋ Make wind sounds, pretending that the winds are building up to a big storm so the sledders need to take cover.

❋ Use your imagination and detail the views you pass by, such as a snow-covered mountain, dogs playing in the snow, or maybe a frozen lake where you might want to get off the sled and take an ice skating break.

❋ Vary the bumpiness of the ride by quickly pulling the blanket forward or slowing it down, or jumble the sled by pulling left or right.

Take turns sharing the fun!

Snowflakes

Decorate your house with snowflakes. Then it'll really feel like winter—even if you're watching a baseball game.

What You Need

❋ White paper

❋ Scissors

❋ Newspaper

❋ Glue

❋ Glitter (optional)

❋ A grown-up to assist

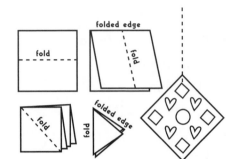

1. Fold the paper in half at least three or four times.
2. Use the scissors to cut out shapes in the paper while folded.
3. Open the paper up.
4. Spread out newspaper on a tabletop.
5. Drip glue onto your snowflake.
6. Sprinkle glitter over the glue.
7. Once the glue is dry you can hang the snowflakes.

You can create a family snowflake by working on each snowflake together—each person makes a cut in the folded paper and then passes it to another person. Each family member can begin a snowflake and then pass it along to others. Compare these snowflakes. How are they similar? How are they different? Just as each family member is unique, so too is each snowflake cutout you create.

Summer in January Night

If you and your family get cabin fever in the middle of winter, you will really benefit from celebrating summer to reduce the fever.

Summertime is a time for dreaming, vacations, fresh food, and outdoor fun. But you don't have to wait six months for these things. Use your imagination and feel the heat. Here are some activities to help turn up the temperature in your home when it's cold outside.

Make Fans

Boy is it hot in here! You'd better make a fan to cool off.

What You Need

* Paper
* Markers
* Stickers
* Glue
* Glitter

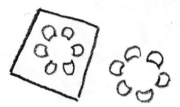

1. Decorate your paper however you like—the more colorful the better. You may want to use summer colors such as bright orange, green, and yellow. Add stickers and/or glue to affix glitter.

2. Once the paper dries completely, place it in front of you and begin folding it lengthwise a 1/2 inch at a time. Turn the paper upside down and repeat to fold it accordion-style or like a fan.

3. Continue until the entire paper is folded. Hold the paper at one end, and fan out the other end. Use it to fan your face.

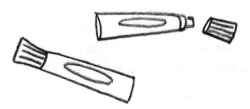

Beach Balloony Ball

What You Need

* 2 chairs or something to represent the net
* Balloon

1. Place the chairs in the middle of the room.

2. Divide into two teams, with one team on each side of the room.

3. Play volleyball using the balloon. Regular volleyball rules apply, but this version is a lot easier because the balloon moves much slower than a volleyball. It's also a lot less dangerous because you're less likely to break anything with a balloon. Still, be careful not to run into each other or into lamps or other breakables while playing.

You can also play Gravity Balloony Ball. In this version of the game, instead of being on separate teams, the whole family works together to keep the ball from touching the floor.

The Brady Bunch, a television show featuring a mother of three girls who marries a father of three boys, ran for five seasons and a total of 117 episodes. One of its most famous quotes: "Mom always said, 'Don't play ball in the house!'"

Tropical Treats

Here are some treats to make your evening feel warm and tropical.

Tropical Punch

Tropical fruit may be out of season in winter, but it's always the right time for a tasty, fruity punch drink.

What You Need

* ❋ Fruit punch
* ❋ Ice
* ❋ Toothpicks (optional)
* ❋ Construction paper
* ❋ Scissors
* ❋ Pineapple, cherries, strawberries, peaches, or other summer fruits you like, fresh or frozen, cut into pieces
* ❋ Glasses, one for each person
* ❋ Stirrers
* ❋ Decorative umbrellas
* ❋ Straws
* ❋ A grown-up to assist

1. Pour the fruit punch into a glass filled with ice.

2. Then add the fruits to the glass. Use a stirrer to mix up the punch.

3. Leave the stirrer inside the glass. Put a few pieces of fruit on a toothpick and put the toothpick in the glass.

4. Cut out fun tropical shapes from construction paper, such as fruits and palm trees. Cut two small slits in the top and bottom of the shape and put a straw through the shape so that the shape sticks out of the top of the glass when the straw is in the glass.

Name your drink something tropical like "Splash on the Beach" or your last name plus "-rita," such as "Kennedyrita."

If you have longer sticks you can make fruit kabobs by piling the pieces of fruit all the way down the stick.

Here are some other tasty treats to get you into a summertime mood:

* ❋ Ice cream—especially banana splits!
* ❋ Grilled hot dogs
* ❋ Cold fried chicken

Pineapple Boat

Slice a pineapple in half and lay the halves down with the fruit side up. Carve out the fruit and make shapes with it. Using toothpicks and shish kabob sticks, place the pineapple fruit chunks back on the pineapple boat like sails or parts of a real boat.

Picnic Party

Here's a simple way to perk up a family dinner—have an indoor picnic in the middle of winter.

What You Need

* A blanket
* Paper plates
* Plastic silverware
* Napkins
* Your dinner
* Lemonade (optional)

To keep them cool in the summer heat, zookeepers freeze the food they give some of their animals. They are fed fish, fruits, and vegetables in big blocks of ice.

1. Spread the blanket on the floor.
2. Set the floor "table" with paper plates, plastic silverware, and napkins.
3. Wear some of your warm-weather clothes such as T-shirts and shorts. (You might want to put socks on to keep your feet warm if you have hardwood or tile floors.)
4. Serve your picnic dinner, and have lemonade with it if you like.

You can even eat some of the tropical treats mentioned earlier in this section to help you get into the summer spirit.

Marco Polo

This is traditionally a swimming pool game, but why not bring it indoors in the middle of winter? Marco Polo is basically a game of tag with a fun twist.

What You Need

❋ An open area, with nothing to trip over or break

❋ A blindfold

1. Choose one family member to be "it."

2. Tie on the blindfold.

3. Spin the blindfolded person around a couple of times. Every time she says, "Marco!" all other family members must say, "Polo!" to let her know where in the room each person is located. She can call out "Marco" as often as she wants until she tags someone.

In Iceland there's sunlight in the summertime 24 hours per day.

Fourth of January

Put on your red, white, and blue clothes and celebrate the half birthday of America! In addition to dressing in these colors, here are some other things you can do to celebrate this half-year holiday:

❋ Draw pictures of fireworks

❋ Have a parade (see Circus Night)

❋ Decorate your home with red, white, and blue streamers

❋ Make and eat only red, white, or blue food

❋ Watch the Schoolhouse Rock! video *Fireworks*

Do you have a summer birthday? Statistically, the fewest births happen in the summer.

Some parades feature bicycle-decorating contests on the Fourth of July. On this half-day holiday, feature a bed-decorating contest. Each family member decorates his or her own bed in a patriotic theme. Use streamers, dress stuffed animals in patriotic colors, and more. See whose bed is the most creative and the most patriotic.

Happy Unbirthday Night

It is nobody's birthday tonight and that's a wonderful reason to have a party! In *Alice in Wonderland*, Alice wanders into a tea party attended by the Mad Hatter, the March Hare, and the Dormouse. They are celebrating their unbirthdays! You can eat cake and ice cream, of course. Just because it's an unbirthday doesn't mean we can't enjoy some tasty treats! You can also play unbirthday games and do unbirthday activities to celebrate your life every day, not just once a year. Enjoy your family's unbirthday party with these fun activities!

Sing the Unbirthday Song

It's not the "Happy Birthday Song"; this is the "Happy Unbirthday Song!"

Happy unbirthday to you and to you
Happy unbirthday to us and me, too
Unbirthdays are fun days to do what we do
So happy unbirthday to you and to you!

Here are some ideas to celebrate your originality, style, and uniqueness while singing the unbirthday song:

❅ Make up your own family dance with hand movements to go along with the song.

❅ Create and wear original unbirthday hats.

❅ Tell what your unbirthday wish would be after you blow out your unbirthday candles.

❅ Sing the song in funny styles such as baby style, cowboy style, or monster style.

> The "Happy Birthday" song is copyrighted, which means that every time it is sung, you must pay a royalty to the copyright holder of this song. That's why many restaurants have written their own song to sing to you when it's your birthday. (But don't worry about singing the traditional song in your home.)

Take the Tail Off the Donkey

Pin the Tail on the Donkey has been a traditional birthday party game throughout the United States and much of Europe for generations. At your unbirthday party, you can play the opposite version of this birthday party classic.

What You Need

❅ Paper
❅ Scissors
❅ Handkerchief
❅ Crayons or markers
❅ Tape
❅ A grown-up to assist

1. Using the crayons or markers, draw and then color a picture of a donkey.

2. Cut off the donkey's tail and then tape it back on with one piece of tape.

3. Tape the donkey drawing with the tail taped onto it to the wall.

4. Use the handkerchief to blindfold a family member. Gently turn around the blindfolded person three times, and then send him off into the direction of the donkey. Now see if he can take the tail off the donkey.

You can also make up your own versions of Pin the Tail on the Donkey. Hang up a photograph of a family member, cut out pictures of funny hats, and play Pin the Hat on Mom. Or play a three-dimensional version using a stuffed animal and a sock as a tail.

> Mark Twain invented a game called Memory Builder. It was a lot like Trivial Pursuit.

Giveaway Non-Presents

You can have an unbirthday grab bag (see Grab Bag Gift Giving on page 123) or give non-presents. Non-presents are different from birthday presents because instead of someone giving them to you, you take them from others.

What You Need

❋ Things to be taken away (see below)

❋ Table

❋ Deck of playing cards

1. Each family member collects three things he or she is willing to give away. Once everyone has selected the items, the game can begin. Each player places the three items in front of him or her at the table where the card game will be played.

2. Choose someone to shuffle and deal the cards.

3. Deal each family member one card facedown.

4. On the count of three each person turns over his or her card. The player with the highest card gets to take one item from the player who has the lowest card. (Face cards are worth more than numbered cards, with jacks the lowest-value face card, kings the highest, and queens are in-between. Aces are ones. If you play with jokers in the deck, these have the highest value of all.)

5. Continue playing until each player wins at least one hand, or play until there is one player remaining with all the presents. Now that's a big unbirthday present game!

The "Happy Birthday" song was the first song to be sung in outer space. Astronauts sang it in 1969.

Create-Your-Own Holiday Night

My daughter once asked me, "What's Casual Plastic Day?" I didn't understand what she meant at first, and then I realized she had heard about Casmir Pulaski Day, a day celebrated in Chicago. Our family thought Casual Plastic Day sounded fun, so we kept that name and have found ways to celebrate it.

For this fun night with the family, create a made-up holiday. It can be about anything in the world. If you have a favorite hobby or type of animal, create a holiday to celebrate it. You can give each other cards for that holiday and create your own traditions. This chapter contains ideas for celebrating your original holiday.

Decorating the Sacred Object

Once you have decided on the type of holiday you want to celebrate, choose an object related to the holiday theme and make it a sacred object by decorating it. For example, trees are decorated for Christmas and eggs for Easter. What can your family decorate for your holiday? Use your imagination. It can be as silly as you want. Here are some examples to inspire you:

✳ On **Casual Plastic Day** we decorate the sacred Tupperware sculpture. We put all of our plastic food containers together in the center of the room and then decorate them with small plastic cups, forks, knives, and spoons.

✳ On **String Cheese Day** we decorate the dairy cow. We draw a big yellow cow and decorate her with cutouts in the shape of milk products.

✳ On **Shoelace Day** we tie shoelaces together and shape them into a giant shoe. And we eat a dinner of food that resembles shoelaces, such as spaghetti and green beans, and licorice for dessert.

> A family on the television show *Seinfeld* celebrated a holiday called Festivus, which is a celebration of all winter holiday celebrations.

New Family Traditions

Each holiday comes with its own set of family traditions. Create some traditions for your family on your made-up holiday.

Here are some ideas for things to wear on your special holiday:

✳ On **Casual Plastic Day** we wear sweat suits (because it's very casual) and we pin plastic toys to our clothes.

✳ On **String Cheese Day** we dress in yellow.

✳ On **Shoelace Day** we wear a lot of shoelaces as necklaces, bracelets, ribbons, and more.

Here are some ideas for foods to eat on your special holiday:

✳ On **Casual Plastic Day** we eat gelatin and gummy candy because it has a plastic consistency.

✳ On **String Cheese Day** we eat a lot of string cheese!

✳ On **Shoelace Day** we bake a cake shaped like a shoe and lace it with licorice sticks.

Here are some ideas for games you can play and songs you can sing on your special holiday:

✳ On **Casual Plastic Day** we play with little plastic people.

✳ On **String Cheese Day**, every time we say a word that starts with the letter M we have to Moo. For example: "Moooooove over Mooooother, I need moooooore room!"

✳ On **Shoelace Day** we play games with our shoes such as Bubble Gum, Bubble Gum in a Dish and we sing "Shoe Fly, Don't Bother Me."

The First Holiday

Every holiday has good stories of love, triumph over hardship, and devotion. You can create your own story for your holiday. Sit around a table with your family and dream up stories, no matter how silly or scary, about the first time your holiday was celebrated.

Here's an example of a made-up story of the first time Casual Plastic Day was celebrated:

Many years ago the workers in a plastic factory were fed up with having to wear formal clothes to work. They chose a day to protest, and they all showed up to work wearing casual clothes. This was the beginning of Casual Plastic Day.

Here's an example of a made-up story of the first time String Cheese Day was celebrated:

Children used to eat their cheese in chunks or bites. But then a magic cow appeared. He said the magic words, Abra Ca Mooooola, and cheese was formed into tubes, which could be pulled apart into strings! Children everywhere rejoiced!

Here's an example of a made-up story of the first time Shoelace Day was celebrated:

Once upon a time shoes kept falling off everyone's feet, and nobody knew what to do. Then Mr. Stu Lace came up with a solution. We now celebrate Shoelace Day in his honor.

Now share true tales of things you did when you celebrated this holiday in previous years with your family. Sharing pictures of these days can be fun, too, or you can draw pictures depicting activities at the previous holidays.

Conclusion

I hope these evenings lead to lasting family bonding and memories for you. They certainly have for me. Don't worry about everything being just right. Sometimes the activities don't go exactly how you planned. Those nights are sometimes more fun and memorable than the ones that went perfectly.

Perhaps the ideas for these family nights will inspire you to create your own family fun nights.

Any way you do it, make sure to spend some enjoyable evenings with your family—there's nothing better!

Resources

Create more family fun with the help of these resources.

Talent Night

Books

Bany-Winters, Lisa. *On Stage: Theater Games and Activities for Kids*. Chicago: Chicago Review Press, 1997.

Bany-Winters, Lisa. *Show Time: Music, Dance, and Drama Activities for Kids*. Chicago: Chicago Review Press, 2000.

Bechdolt, Jack. *Little Boy with a Big Horn*. New York: Golden Books, 1999.

Krull, Kathleen. *M Is for Music*. New York: Harcourt Children's Books, 2003.

Rittenhouse, Barbara, and Leigh Anna Reichenbach. *Santa's Pants Are Falling Down and Other Silly Songs of the Season*. New York: Scholastic, Inc., 2004.

Sesame Street. *Elmo Plays Piano*. Lincolnwood, IL: Publications International, Ltd., 2001. (Comes with a keyboard.)

Sesame Street. *Elmo's Jumpin' Jukebox*. Lincolnwood, IL: Publications International, Ltd., 2004. (This book even comes with a microphone.)

Winter, Jonah. *Once Upon a Time in Chicago: The Story of Benny Goodman*. New York: Hyperion, 2000.

Videos/DVDs

Disney Sing-Along Videos. All are great resources; various years. Disney Studios.

Fantasia. Disney Studios, 1942.

Fantasia 2000. Disney Studios, 2000.

The Nutcracker. Warner Studios, 2004. (This New York City Ballet version is very family friendly.)

Web Sites

Dallas Symphony Orchestra. www.dsokids.com. Orchestra information.

Enchanted Learning. www.enchantedlearning.com/crafts/music. Information on how to make more musical instruments.

Circus Night

Books

Ehlert, Lois. *Circus*. New York: HarperCollins, 1992.

Falconer, Ian. *Olivia Saves the Circus*. New York: Atheneum/Anne Schwartz Books, 2001.

Redbank, Tennant. *Jojo's Circus: Clown School*. New York: Disney Press, 2005.

Videos/DVDs

Cirque du Soleil. Any of their shows. Columbia Tristar.

Jojo's Circus: Take a Bow. Buena Vista Home Video, 2005.

Web Sites

Cirque du Soleil. www.cirquedusoleil.com. This is the site for a very different and artistic circus.

Ringling Brothers Circus. www.ringling.com. This is the official Ringling Brothers Circus Web site.

Poetry Slam Night

Books

Dr. Seuss. *Oh Say Can You Say?* New York: Random House, 1979.

Koch, Kenneth, and Kate Farrell, eds. *Talking to the Sun: An Illustrated Anthology of Poems for Young People*. New York: Henry Holt & Co, 1985.

Martin, Bill Jr., and John Archambault. *Chicka Chicka Boom Boom*. New York: Aladdin, 2000.

Mother Goose nursery rhyme books. Any.

Nash, Ogden. *The Tale of Custard the Dragon*. New York: Little, Brown, 1998.

Perkins, Al. *Hand, Hand, Fingers, Thumb*. New York: Random House, 1969.

Prelutsky, Jack. Any of his wonderful poetry books.

Videos/DVDs

Alice in Wonderland. Walt Disney Home Video, 2004.

A Midsummer Night's Dream. Twentieth-Century Fox, 2003.

Web Sites

Giggle Poetry. www.gigglepoetry.com. Funny kid-friendly poems.

Poetry for Kids. www.poetry4kids.com. Family poems.

Movie Star Night

Books

Brown, Jordan (Ghostwriter). *Movie Marvels: Film Facts You'll Flip For*. Welwyn: Hertfordshire, 1995.

Disney Press. *The Disney Poster: The Animated Film Classics from Mickey Mouse to Aladdin*. New York: Disney Editions, 1993.

Hamilton, Tisha, adapter. *Disney Pixar Amazing Adventures Movie Theater Storybook and Movie Projector*. New York: Reader's Digest, 2004.

Videos/DVDs

The Muppet Movie. Columbia/Tristar Studios, 2001.

Scene It DVD Game. Mattel. (In my family we especially love the Disney and Harry Potter editions).

Web Sites

Academy of Motion Picture Arts and Sciences. www.oscars.org. Fun trivia and history on Academy Awards.

Movie Goods. www.moviegoods.com. Various movie information.

Giggle Night

Books

Bany-Winters, Lisa. *Funny Bones: Comedy Games and Activities for Kids*. Chicago: Chicago Review Press, 2002.

Dahl, Michael. *The Everything Kids' Joke Book: Side-Splitting, Rib-Tickling Fun*. Everything Kids Series. Avon, MA: Adams Media Corporation, 2002.

Mad Libs. Any. New York: Price Stern Sloan.

Parish, Peggy. All Amelia Bedelia books. New York: HarperTrophy.

Scieszka, Jon, and Lane Smith. *The Stinky Cheese Man*. New York: Viking, 1992.

Weintraub, Eileen. *The Everything Kids' Knock Knock Book: Jokes Guaranteed to Leave Your Friends in Stitches*. Everything Kids Series. Avon, MA: Adams Media Corporation, 2004.

Videos/DVDs

Silly Symphonies. Disney Studios, 2001 (DVD).

Pee Wee's Playhouse. Image Entertainment, 2004.

Web Sites

AZ Kids Net. www.azkidsnet.com. Jokes for kids.

Kids Domain. www.kidsdomain.com. Jokes and many other things kids would enjoy.

Jokes for Kids. www.jokesforkids.com.

Sticky Icky Night

Books

Branzei, Sylvia, and Jack Keely. *Grossology*. New York: Price Stern Sloan, 2002.

Masoff, Joy. *Oh, Yuck: The Encyclopedia of Everything Nasty*. New York: Workman Publishing Company, 2000.

Videos/DVDs

Bill Nye the Science Guy. Any video. Disney Studios.

Web Sites

The Yuckiest Site on the Internet. http://yucky.kids.discovery.com. Some yucky science information.

Splash Night

Books

Locker, Thomas. *Water Dance*. Orlando, FL: Harcourt Brace & Company, 1997.

Robinson, Tom. *The Everything Kids' Science Experiments Book: Boil Ice, Float Water, Measure Gravity—Challenge the World Around You!* Everything Kids Series. Avon, MA: Adams Media Corporation, 2001.

Wagner, Kathi, and Obe Wagner. *The Everything Kids' Sharks Book: Dive into Fun-Infested Waters!* Everything Kids Series. Avon, MA: Adams Media Corporation, 2005.

Videos/DVDs

Finding Nemo. Disney Pixar, 2001.
The Little Mermaid. Buena Vista Home Video, 1990.
Shark Tale. Dreamworks, 2005.
The SpongeBob SquarePants Movie. Paramount Home Video, 2005.

Web Sites

Water Education Foundation. www.water-ed.org. Interesting and educational water information and experiments.

Opposite Night

Books

Dr. Seuss. *The Foot Book*. New York: Random House, 1968.

Videos/DVDs

Big. Twentieth-Century Fox, 2003 (on DVD).
Freaky Friday. Walt Disney Home Video, 2004.

Animal Night

Books

Base, Graeme. *Animalia*. New York: Harry N. Abrams, 1987.

Carle, Eric. *Animals Animals*. New York: Philomel Books, 1989. (Most of his books are about animals, and all are wonderful!)

Discovery Communications Inc. *Animalogy: Weird and Wacky Animal Facts*. Animal Planet. New York: Knopf, 1998.

Morris, Johnny. *Animal Go Round*. New York: DK Publications, 2001.

Sams, Carl R. II, and Jean Stoick. *Stranger in the Woods*. Milford, MI: Carl R. Sams II Photography, 1999.

Videos/DVDs

The Bear. Columbia TriStar Studios, 2004.
Dr. Dolittle. Twentieth-Century Fox, 2003.
The Jungle Book. Disney Studios, 1999 (DVD).
The Lion King. Walt Disney Home Video, 2003 (DVD).
Madagascar. Universal Studios, 2005.

Web Sites

Animal Planet. www.animal.discovery.com. Fun, kid-friendly information on animals.

National Geographic. www.nationalgeographic.com/kids. Fabulous photographs and animal facts.

Switcheroo Zoo. www.switchzoo.com. You can create your own animals here!

Indoor Garden Night

Books

Carlson, Laurie. *Green Thumbs: A Kid's Activity Guide to Indoor and Outdoor Gardening*. Chicago: Chicago Review Press, 1995.

Scheer, Julian, and Marvin Bileck. *Rain Makes Applesauce*. New York: Holiday House, 1964.

Videos/DVDs

Linnea in Monet's Garden. First Run Features, 1996.

Melody Time. Walt Disney Home Video, 2000. (Contains *Johnny Appleseed*.)

Web Sites

Global Garden. www.global-garden.com.au/gardenkids.htm. Includes kid-friendly information and gardening tips.

Kids Gardening. www.kidsgardening.com. A lot of gardening ideas and activities.

Science Night

Books

All DK Eyewitness Books. New York: DK Children.

Cole, Joanna. Magic School Bus Series. New York: Scholastic Press.

Videos/DVDs

Bill Nye the Science Guy. Any video. Disney Studios.

Honey, I Shrunk the Kids. Walt Disney Home Video, 2005 (DVD).

School House Rock: Science Rock. Walt Disney Home Video, 2002 (DVD).

Web Sites

Cool Science for Curious Kids. www.hhmi.org/coolscience. Cool science experiments.

Science for Kids. www.sciencenewsforkids.org. Fun scientific news and ideas.

For Kids Only: Earth Science Enterprise. http://kids.earth.nasa.gov. The official Web site for NASA space travel.

Spa Night

Books

Lerner, Harriet, and Susan Goldhor. *Franny B. Kranny, There's a Bird in Your Hair!* New York: Harper Collins, 2001.

Traig, Jennifer, and Julianne Balmain. *Beauty Things to Make and Do*. San Francisco: Chronicle Books, 2001.

Wallace, Mary, Jessica Wallace, and Claudia Davila. *The Girls' Spa Book: Twenty Dreamy Ways to Relax and Feel Great*. Toronto, Ontario, Canada: Maple Tree Press, 2004.

Videos/DVDs

The Princess Diaries. Walt Disney Home Entertainment, 2005.

Web Sites

Foot Candy. www.footcandy.com. Pedicure and foot fun, as well as other spa recipes.

Reflexology Directory. www.reflexology-directory.com. Pressure point charts, foot massage information and more.

Shantala Massage. www.shantalamassage.org. Contains instructions for baby and child massage.

Formal Night

Books

Alison, Marielle, and Liza Woodruff. *How to Be a Bride and a Flower Girl, Too*. New York: Little Simon, 1999.

Brown, Marc. *D.W. Thinks Big*. New York: Little, Brown, 1995.

Cheshire, Marc, and Chris Hahner. *Eloise Dresses Up*. New York: Little Simon, 2005.

Kirk, David. *Miss Spider's Wedding*. New York: Scholastic Press, 1995.

Videos/DVDs

Cinderella. Walt Disney Home Entertainment, 2005 (DVD).

Royal Wedding. Goodtimes Home Video, 2001 (DVD). (Fred Astaire dances on the ceiling!)

Top Hat. RKO Collection, 1935.

Web Sites

Ballroom Dancers. www.ballroomdancers.com. Dance terminology, positions, and interesting information on waltzing and other ballroom dance styles.

Masquerade: www.masqueradevenetianmasks.com. Handmade Venetian Masks. Contains the history of Venetian Carnival masks, as well as pictures of amazing masquerade masks.

Jewelry Night

Books

American Girl. *Doll Jewelry: Make Bracelets, Necklaces, Anklets, and More*. Middleton, WI: American Girl, 2005.

Peduzzi, Kelli. *Paper Clip Jewelry: A Paper Clip Jewelry Workshop*. American Girl Library. Middleton, WI: Pleasant Company Publications, 2000.

Torres, Laura. *Friendship Bracelets*. Palo Alta, CA: Klutz, 1996.

Web Sites

About Style: Jewelry/Accessories. www.jewelrymaking.about.com. Instructions for a lot of jewelry projects.

All About Colored Gemstones. www.gemstone.org. Contains birthstone information and interesting facts about gemstones.

Spooky Night

Books

Dr. Seuss. *The Sneetches and Other Stories*. New York: Random House, 1961. (It contains "What Was I Scared Of," my family's favorite spooky story!)

Morgan, Melissa, and Heidi Cho. *The Polar Express: The Movie; Shadowbook*. Boston: Houghton Mifflin, 2004.

Stone, Jon, and Michael Smollin. *The Monster at the End of This Book*. New York: Golden Books, 2003.

Western Pub Group. Dare You Go Series. New York: Golden Books.

Videos/DVDs

Addams Family Values. Paramount Studio, 2003 (DVD).

Goosebumps—any of the videos. Fox Home Entertainment. (Be careful, these are pretty scary!)

The Haunted Mansion. Walt Disney Home Video, 2005.

The Witches. Warner Studios, 2004 (DVD).

Web Sites

Halloween Ghost Stories. www.halloweenghoststories.com. Includes classic stories like "The Legend of Sleepy Hollow" by Washington Irving and "The Tell-Tale Heart" by Edgar Allen Poe. Also contains new and original ghost stories.

Haunted Dog House. www.haunteddoghouse.com. Fun kid-friendly spooky site hosted by a cute dog.

Little Folks: Fun for Kids Big and Small: The Shadow-Fun Page. www.little-folks.com/hand_shadows/hand_shadows_01.htm. Provides information on hand shadows you can make.

Fortune-Telling Night

Books

Girls Club Fortune Telling Kit. Philadelphia: Running Press Book Publishers, 2001.

Stewig, John Warren, and Margo Tomes. *The Fisherman and His Wife*. New York: Holiday House, 1988.

Videos/DVDs

Django Legacy. Vestapol Videos, 2004. (Amazing Gypsy guitar music.)

Harry Potter and the Sorcerer's Stone. Warner Home Video, 2005.

The Hunchback of Notre Dame. Disney Studios, 2005 (DVD).

Web Sites

Orderly Fashionable Experience, The. www.ofesite.com. Palm reading charts, horoscopes, and much more.

Sanrio Fortune Corner, to get your Chinese zodiac fortune. www.sanrio.com/main/zodiac/chinese/chinmain.html.

Kids Chat: Daily Horoscopes for Kids. www.kidschat.net/horoscopes.html.

Get your Hello Kitty fortune here. www.sanrio.com/main/zodiac/zodiacmain.html.

Mystery Night

Books

Emberley, Ed. *Ed Emberley's Fingerprint Drawing Book*. New York: Little, Brown, 2001.

Marzollo, Jean, and Walter Wick. I Spy books. New York: Cartwheel.

Sobol, Donald J. *Two-Minute Mysteries*. New York: Scholastic Paperbacks, 1991.

Wiese, Jim. *Spy Science: 40 Secret-Sleuthing, Code-Cracking, Spy-Catching Activities for Kids*. Hoboken, NJ: John Wiley & Sons, Inc., 2001.

Videos/DVDs

Clue. Paramount Studio, 2004 (DVD). (For older kids. Goes great with the game!)

Scooby-Doo. Warner Home Video, 2004.

Wishbone: The Slobbery Hound. Lyrick Studio Video, 1996.

Web Sites

Candlelight Stories. www.candlelightstories.com. Contains stories plus a kids mystery writing contest!

Mystery Net's Kids Mysteries. http://kids.mysterynet.com. Contains mysteries the entire family can solve, plus spooky stories and magic tricks.

Scrapbook Night

Books

Kids Can Press puts out a series of "Memory Scrapbooks for Kids" that include family members like "My Baby Brother and Me" as well as school experiences like "My Class and Me." www.kidscanpress.com.

Web Sites

Archiver's: The Photo Memory Store. www.archiversonline.com. Contains a section on scrapbook ideas, information on classes you can take, and scrapbook materials you can purchase.

Precious Memories: My Scrapbook. www.myscrapbookshop.com. Also contains a section of terrific layout ideas.

Family History Night

Books

Hartley, William G. *The Everything Family Tree Book: Finding, Charting, and Preserving Your Family History*. Avon, MA: Adams Media Corporation, 1997.

Taylor, Maureen A. *Through the Eyes of Your Ancestors*. New York: Houghton Mifflin, 1999.

Wolfman, Ira. *Climbing Your Family Tree*. New York: Workman Publishing Company, 2002.

Videos/DVDs

Little Women. Columbia Tristar Studios, 2003 (DVD).

Web Sites

Geneology Web: Family Name History; Find Your Ancient Family Roots. www.geneologyweb.com/familyhistory.htm. Type in your last name and find out history, coat of arms, connections, and castles related to your ancestors.

Family Tree Magazine. www.familytreemagazine.com. The Web site for a magazine devoted to family histories.

Trains, Planes, and Automobiles Night

Books

Fisher-Price. *Songs That Go*. East Aurora, NY: Fisher-Price, 1999.

Phidal. *Things That Go!* Montreal, Ontario, Canada: Phidal Publishing, Inc., 2001.

Priddy, Roger. *My Big Train Book*. New York: St. Martin's Press, 2003.

Videos/DVDs

Herbie—Fully Loaded. Buena Vista Home Video, 2005.
The Little Engine That Could. Universal Studios, 1993.
The Polar Express. Warner Home Video, 2005 (DVD).

Web Sites

Airplanes for Kids. www.airplanesforkids.com. A kid-friendly airplane site, with a lot of information on airplanes of all sorts.

Thomas and Friends. www.hitentertainment.com/thomasandfriends. For games, activities, and information on Thomas the Tank Engine and Friends.

Scavenger Hunt Night

Books

Handford, Martin. *Where's Waldo?* The Wonder Book. Cambridge, MA: Candlewick, 1997.

Marzollo, Jane. *I Spy Fun House: A Picture Book of Riddles*. New York: Cartwheel, 1993.

Videos/DVDs

Into the Woods. Image Entertainment, 1997.

Web Sites

Haley Productions. "Do It Yourself Scavenger Hunts." www.scavenger-hunt-idea.com. Many ideas that can be downloaded for different kids of scavenger hunts.

Point Isabel ISD: Scavenger Hunts. www.pi-isd.net/scavengerhunts.htm. Great educational scavenger hunts including Animals of the World and Geography hunts.

Winter in July Night

Books

Carle, Eric. *Dream Snow*. New York: Philomel, 2000.

Plourde, Lynn. *Winter Waits*. New York: Simon & Schuster, 2001.

Rittenhouse, Barbara, and Leigh Anna Reichenbach. *Santa's Pants Are Falling Down and Other Silly Songs of the Season*. New York: Scholastic, Inc., 2004.

Sams, Carl R. II, and Jean Stoick. *Stranger in the Woods*. Milford, MI: Carl R. Sams II Photography, 1999.

Videos/DVDs

Elf. New Line Home Entertainment, 2005 (DVD).

The Grinch. Universal Studios, 2003 (DVD).

The Nightmare Before Christmas. Touchstone Video, 1997.

The Nutcracker. Warner Studios, 2004 on (DVD). (This New York City Ballet version is very family friendly and a favorite at our house.)

The Polar Express. Warner Home Video, 2005 (DVD).

The Snowman. Columbia/Tristar Studios, 2004.

Web Sites

Claus.com. www.claus.com. Check your naughty/nice rating plus other fun seasonal activities.

Gingerbread Lane. www.gingerbreadlane.com. Provides ideas on how to make gingerbread houses and even a gingerbread train.

Kids Domain: Online Winter Games. www.kidsdomain.com/games/winter.html. Fun winter-themed games including Evil Elves, Snowball Toss, and a chance to design a snowman.

Santa's Secret Village. www.northpole.com. Play seasonal games or send a letter to Santa.

Summer in January Night

Books

Kennedy, Jimmy, and Day, Alexandra. *Teddy Bears' Picnic*. New York: Aladdin, 2000.

Plourde, Lynn. *Summer's Vacation*. New York: Simon & Schuster, 2003.

Videos/DVDs

Addams Family Values. Paramount Studio, 2003 (DVD).

The Parent Trap. Disney Studios, 2004.

School House Rock: America Rock. Walt Disney Home Video, 2002 (DVD).

Web Sites

Kids Domain: Holiday Fun; Summer. www.kidsdomain.com/games/summer.html. Ideas for fun activities on all summer holidays including the Fourth of July, Flag Day, Father's Day, etc.

Happy Unbirthday Night

Books

Goldberg, Whoopi. *Alice*. New York: Bantam, 1992.

Prelutsky, Jack, and Lane Smith. *Dr. Seuss' Hooray for Diffendoofer Day*. New York: Knopf, 1998.

Sabuda, Robert, and Lewis Carroll. *Alice's Adventures in Wonderland: A Pop-Up Adaptation*. New York: Little Simon, 2003.

Videos/DVDs

Alice in Wonderland. Walt Disney Home Video, 2004.

Gus. Disney Studios, 2003.

Web Sites

Kids Parties Connection. "Birthday Traditions from Around the World." www.kidsparties.com/traditions.htm. A history of birthday parties, traditions from other countries, and a list of what famous people share your birthday (and your unbirthday).

A Kid's Heart. www.akidsheart.com. Contains online birthday games including Pin the Tail on the Donkey.

Create-Your-Own-Holiday Night

Books

DK Publishing. *DK Readers: Holiday! Celebration Days from Around the World*. New York: DK Children, 2000.

Jones, Linda. *Kids Around the World Celebrate: The Best Feasts and Festivals from Many Lands*. Hoboken, NJ: John Wiley & Sons, 1999.

Kindersly, Anabel, and Barnabas Kindersly. *Children Just Like Me: Celebrations!* New York: DK Children, 1997.

Videos/DVDs

Holiday Inn. Universal Studios, 2004 (DVD).

Web Sites

Holidays from Around the World. www.zuzu.org/daze.html. Memories, experiences, special reports, and stories about holiday celebrations from all over the world.

Multi-Cultural Calendar. www.kidlink.org/KIDPROJ/MCC. This site has information on common and uncommon holidays like Potato Day (October) and Thinking Day (February).

Bibliography

Acupressure. "Acupressure Points." www.online-matrimonials.com/acupr/Acupressure%20point.html (accessed August 9, 2005).

Anonymous. "P.T. Barnum," *Encyclopedia Britannica*, 11th ed., Vol. III, Cambridge University Press, 1910, quoted in Theatrehistory.com/american/barnum001.html.

Circus Present and Past. www.circusweb.com (accessed August 9, 2005).

Cool Quiz. "Trivia Directory." http://coolquiz.com/trivia (accessed August 31, 2005).

Duncan, Stephen F. "Family Strengths: Time Together." Forever Families. www.foreverfamilies.net/xml/articles/time_together.aspx?&publication=short (accessed August 9, 2005).

Fire Lady's Garden "Months—Birthstones and Meanings and Flowers." www.geocities.com/Heartland/Village/3491/monthsstonesmeaning.html (accessed August 9, 2005).

Healing Hands Massage Therapy. "Foot Reflexology: Healing Through Pressure Therapy." www.healinghandsinc.com/reflexology.htm.

History of Fingerprints, The. http://onin.com/fp/fphistory.html (accessed August 31, 2005).

Jewelry Mae. "Days of the Week Stones." www.jewelrymae.com/gfdays.html (accessed August 31, 2005).

Kindersley, Barnabas, and Anabel Kindersley. *Children Just Like Me: Celebrations!* New York: DK Publishing, Inc., 1997.

North-Jones, Peggy. "Preserving Family Time." Mom Central, online newsletter. www.momcentral.com/smuartfamily.htm (accessed May 18, 2004).

Orderly Fashionable Experience, The. "The Lines." www.ofesite.com/spirit/palm/lines.htm (accessed August 31, 2005).